D1548762

Also by Betty Rohde

So Fat, Low Fat, No Fat

More So Fat, Low Fat, No Fat

Italian So Fat, Low Fat, No Fat

Mexican So Fat, Low Fat, No Fat

So Fat, Low Fat, No Fat Desserts

More than 160 recipes
from the bestselling author
of *So Fat, Low Fat, No Fat*

Betty Rohde

A FIRESIDE BOOK
Published by Simon & Schuster

FIRESIDE
Rockefeller Center
1230 Avenue of the Americas
New York, NY 10020

FIRESIDE and colophon are registered trademarks
of Simon & Schuster Inc.

Designed by Judy Wong

Manufactured in the United States of America

1   3   5   7   9   10   8   6   4   2

Library of Congress Cataloging-in-Publication Data

Rohde, Betty.
So fat, low fat, no fat desserts : more than 160 recipes from the
bestselling author of So fat, low fat, no fat / Betty Rohde.
p.   cm.
"A Fireside Book."
Includes index.
1. Low-fat diet—Recipes.   2. Desserts.   I. Title.
RM237.7.R6284   1999
641.5'638—dc21   98-26413
                                                            CIP

ISBN 0-684-83526-6

Jo Bob

 Well, honey, here we are, book number five and you're still alive.
Who would ever think, I would be up to my ears in ink?

We have traveled the country via our kitchen, from Oklahoma to Italy to Mexico.

Your favorite is Desserts as we all know,

But with So Fat, Low Fat, No Fat Desserts, it doesn't even show.

In February we were married 25 years.

You married me again with tears of love dripping from your cheeks.

It feels like the first time we said "I do" was only a matter of weeks.

Five kids, six grandchildren, three houses, a cabin, a trailer, seven cars, a van & four dogs

I think that makes us tied until they call in the hogs.

Will you say "I do" again in 25 more years?

I will be waiting but if you get there before I do, don't worry,

I will be there as soon as I get through with my chores.

Eternal Love,
Betty

CONTENTS

INTRODUCTION

I shall start this introduction by saying "Hello." My name is Betty Rohde and I am happy to meet you. I hope this is not your first *So Fat, Low Fat, No Fat* cookbook. If it is, I hope you enjoy reading and cooking from my book just a tiny bit as much as I enjoyed researching, cooking, eating, and losing weight during this time. My friends really enjoyed this book (I use them as samplers).

I will tell you about a portion of research I did in New York City at several French restaurants. Now, that was some research, to die for. No, I didn't gain any weight, I was careful all the next day after enjoying the French cuisine. I wish I could just begin to tell you about the desserts Marie and I had. Marie is my friend who travels with me on occasion. She ordered a chocolate soufflé. They have a pastry chef who does nothing but make these desserts while you're eating your dinner. If you are ordering a dessert soufflé you should do that at the time you order your dinner. That soufflé was the most outstanding thing we ate on the entire trip. I have never tasted anything that good, and you won't find a recipe in this book for French soufflé either. I wouldn't even try to begin on one. For the first thing, French cooking is FAT-FULL. There is so much butter in everything, wow—and how good.

I ordered a dessert with the least fattening ingredients:

sherbet. It was large, beautiful, and presented like no one could imagine, and I ate it. Yummy? Well, there is no recipe for that one in this book either. We were just looking and shopping at the time. But we did touch just a little. Ate just a little. OK—ate just a lot. But I don't do it all the time and over and over. That is what puts the weight on and keeps adding pounds: repetitiveness. You should never tell yourself that you're never going to eat that cake or whatever again; you know you are and are lying to yourself if you do say it. But if you do eat something fat-full, just be extra careful the next day or two, depending on how much fun you had.

Our trip was very successful. I got a lot of ideas about different tastes, a lot of ideas of how to put different fruits with different flavors, mix and match, so I again hope you enjoy your new dessert book. Let's get cooking!

SUBSTITUTIONS AND TIPS

Substitute Cocoa for Baking Chocolate

Use 3 tablespoons of cocoa powder and 2 teaspoons of water or coffee for each ounce of baking chocolate.

To Rescue Runny Fat-Free Cream Cheese Frosting

A solution to help when fat-free frosting gets too thin (because of the water base, it breaks down very quickly and easily): Add a couple tablespoons of instant pudding mix to thicken.

For Moist Cakes

Substitute applesauce for oil in cookies, cakes, and brownies. Other purées may be substituted also, such as baby food, bananas, prune purée, and many others.

Substitute a mashed banana or puréed apricots or peaches for the oil in a yellow cake mix.

Substituting Honey for Sugar

By substituting honey for part of the sugar, you get a nice golden glow to your baked goods, and your breads and cakes will stay fresh longer.

You may substitute honey for up to half the sugar called for in a recipe for baked goods. When substituting honey, reduce the amount of liquid by half the amount of honey—for example, if the recipe calls for 2 cups sugar and 1 cup water or milk, and you want to use 1 cup honey and 1 cup sugar, use ½ cup water or milk instead of 1 cup. In a recipe that calls for yeast, add ½ teaspoon of baking soda for each cup of honey used. To prevent overbrowning, lower the oven temperature by 25 degrees.

Baking with Low-Fat or Fat-Free Margarine

The rumor is that you can't bake with low-fat or fat-free margarine. You know if you have any of my books and have read any of my articles that is just like waving a *red flag* in front of me.

I have found that if I use a small amount of light margarine and a larger amount of fat-free, my baking turns out fine. Remember, if it calls for ¾ cup, use ¼ cup light and ½ cup fat-free; or for even better results use ¼ cup regular and ½ cup light.

Solid-type fat-free margarine comes in a plastic tublike container. "Pourable" means squeeze type, pour type, or spray type. Light margarine or lower-fat margarine comes in sticks.

You will need to be the judge of what type you choose. If you are really holding true to a number of fat grams per day, that will be your deciding factor. If you are trying to maintain your diet and cook healthfully for your family, you may choose to go the second route.

Avoid Overbaking

Do not overbake lower-fat baked items. Be sure to start checking for doneness about 10 to 15 minutes before the end of the baking time.

- Keep a can of frozen apple juice concentrate in the door of your freezer with the lid on. You can just dip out a tablespoon of frozen concentrate any time you need it when baking, or you can add it to sauces and/or gravies for a little extra flavor and a little less fat.

- Keep fat-free frozen whipped topping in your freezer for anytime fix-its. You can heal a multitude of sins with a tub of whipped topping. Thicken if too thin, thin if too thick, help stand up if runny, build up portions, stretch amounts, fluff, puff, and stuff. Who could live without frozen whipped topping in their household staples?

- Add three or four drops of peppermint oil to your dishwater when entertaining during the holidays. It really makes your house smell nice—but then it is nice for your house to smell nice any time of the year. You may also add a couple drops of lemon oil for a fresh clean smell, or a couple drops of apple oil or vanilla oil when you're just needing a lift.

- Stock your pantry with cans of the fruit pie filling of your choice. You can always whip up a wonder of wonders in a matter of minutes when you need to look like Julia and you have been shopping all day.

KITCHEN POTPOURRI

3 cups water
Skin of 1 orange
Skin of 1 lemon
Skin of 1 apple
¾ tablespoon whole cloves or allspice

Bring all the ingredients to a boil in a saucepan and turn the heat down to a simmer. Or place in a ceramic container over a candle. It will keep your kitchen citrus-fresh and clean-smelling during your entertaining. I put my potpourri in a teakettle and set it on the wood-burning stove after it starts to boil. Very cozy.

Note: Keep the skins of the above-mentioned fruits in a plastic bag and freeze until needed. You don't need to make a trip to the market to get one or the other just for the skin.

Coffee Cakes, Quick Breads, Muffins, and Sweet Rolls

COFFEE CAKE

1¾ cups Bran Buds
1⅓ cups all-purpose flour
⅔ cup sugar
Pinch of salt (optional)
1 tablespoon baking powder
½ cup egg substitute
1⅓ cups fat-free milk
⅓ cup plus 1 tablespoon applesauce
1 apple, peeled, cored, and chopped very fine

2.25 grams
fat per
serving

Serves 10

Prep   :45
Cook   :50
Stand   :40
Total   2:15

Preheat the oven to 350 degrees. Lightly coat a 9 x 5 x 3-inch loaf pan with vegetable oil cooking spray. Dust with flour and tap out the excess.

In a food processor or blender, crush the Bran Buds to a fine powder. Be patient—this may take 3 or 4 minutes.

Pour the crushed Bran Buds into a mixing bowl. Add the flour, sugar, salt, and baking powder; blend with a wire whisk.

In a separate bowl, combine the egg substitute, milk, and applesauce. Add to the dry ingredients and blend with a whisk or hand-held mixer until smooth. Stir in the apples.

Pour into the prepared pan and bake for 50 to 60 minutes or until the loaf is springy to the touch and pulls slightly from the sides of the pan. Cool in the pan for 10 minutes, then turn out onto a rack and cool completely.

(recipe continues)

Variation:

> *Replace the applesauce with mashed pumpkin during the fall season. If desired, add a pinch of nutmeg and cinnamon.*

MAKE-AHEAD COFFEE CAKE

Assemble this cake the night before and pop it in the oven the next morning.

1 gram fat per serving	
Serves 6	
Prep	:16
Cook	:40
Stand	8:00
Total	8:56

1⅓ cups all-purpose flour
1 teaspoon baking powder
½ teaspoon baking soda
Pinch of salt
1⅓ cups bran flakes cereal with raisins
½ cup plus 2 tablespoons packed brown sugar
1 cup low-fat buttermilk
¼ cup pourable fat-free margarine
¼ cup egg substitute
½ teaspoon ground cinnamon

Lightly spray an 8-inch round or square baking pan with vegetable oil cooking spray.

Combine the flour, baking powder, baking soda, and salt in a bowl. Stir to blend well. Mix in the bran flakes, ½ cup of the brown sugar, and the buttermilk. Stir the margarine and egg substitute together and add to the batter. Continue to stir just until moistened.

Spread the batter in the prepared baking dish. Cover with plastic wrap and refrigerate overnight.

For the topic, mix the remaining 2 tablespoons of brown sugar with the cinnamon and set aside until time to bake.

When ready to bake, preheat the oven to 375 degrees. Uncover the baking dish, sprinkle the topping mix over evenly, and bake for 30 to 40 minutes or until the cake is springy to the touch and pulls slightly from the sides of the pan. Let cool briefly in the pan; serve warm.

QUICK APPLE BREAKFAST CAKE

Excellent with hot tea or coffee at a ladies' morning bridge game. So quick, so easy, yet so good and so fat-free.

1 package fat-free snack cake mix, apple flavor
¾ cup water
2 tablespoons frozen apple juice concentrate
1 to 2 Granny Smith apples, peeled, cored, and sliced in half moons
Ground cinnamon (optional)
Powdered sugar for garnish

Preheat the oven to 350 degrees. Lightly coat a 9-inch round cake pan with vegetable oil cooking spray.

Put the cake mix in a bowl and add the water mixed with apple juice concentrate. Mix with a wire whisk until smooth. Pour the batter into the prepared pan.

Arrange thinly sliced apples over the batter in a full circle design, turning all the slices the same way. Push down

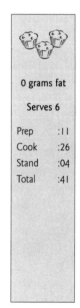

0 grams fat

Serves 6

Prep	:11
Cook	:26
Stand	:04
Total	:41

just a tiny bit on the slices to put them down into the batter about halfway.

Sprinkle with cinnamon if desired. Bake for 26 minutes or until a toothpick inserted in the center comes out clean. Serve warm.

Sprinkle with powdered sugar just before serving if desired.

APPLE COFFEE CAKE

1.25 grams
fat per
serving

Serves 8

Prep   :40
Cook   :40
Stand   :05
Total   1:25

1¾ cups all-purpose flour
¾ cup granulated sugar
¾ teaspoon baking powder
1 teaspoon baking soda
Pinch of salt (optional)
½ teaspoon ground cinnamon
¾ cup low-fat buttermilk
½ cup egg substitute
½ cup applesauce
1 teaspoon vanilla extract
1 cup peeled and finely chopped apple
¼ cup raisins (optional)
¼ cup nuts, chopped fine (optional)

STREUSEL

3 tablespoons brown sugar
1 tablespoon all-purpose flour
¼ cup dry rolled oats
½ teaspoon cinnamon
2 teaspoons low-fat margarine

Preheat the oven to 350 degrees.

Coat an 11 x 7-inch baking dish lightly with vegetable oil cooking spray and dust with flour. Shake excess flour out and set the pan aside.

Combine in a large bowl the flour, granulated sugar, baking powder, baking soda, salt, and cinnamon. Blend with a wire whisk until evenly mixed.

In a separate small bowl, combine the buttermilk, egg substitute, applesauce, and vanilla.

Add the buttermilk mixture to the dry ingredients, mixing until smooth and well blended. Fold in the apples, raisins, and nuts if desired. Pour the batter into the prepared pan.

For the streusel, combine brown sugar, 1 tablespoon flour, the oats, ½ teaspoon cinnamon, and the low-fat margarine. Stir with a fork or mixer until moistened. Sprinkle the streusel over the cake batter. Bake for 35 to 40 minutes or until done to the toothpick test. Let stand about 5 minutes and serve warm with coffee or tea. You can also drizzle a powdered sugar glaze over if using for entertaining. Looks prettier.

Variations:

   If desired you may slice an additional apple in half-moon slices and arrange them in a circle on top of the cake before sprinkling the streusel over.

   Mix ½ cup powdered sugar, 1 tablespoon cold or hot coffee, and 1 teaspoon Kahlua (optional). You can add milk or coffee for added moisture if needed. Let cake cool for 10 minutes. During this time make your *glaze. Pour over hot cake. Serve the cake warm with fat-free ice cream or fat-free frozen yogurt.*

BANANA SOUR CREAM COFFEE CAKE

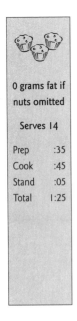

0 grams fat if
nuts omitted

Serves 14

Prep	:35
Cook	:45
Stand	:05
Total	1:25

½ cup solid-type fat-free margarine
1 cup plus ¼ cup granulated sugar
½ cup egg substitute
1 cup mashed bananas (about 2 large)
½ teaspoon vanilla extract
½ cup fat-free sour cream
2 cups all-purpose flour
1 teaspoon baking powder
1 teaspoon baking soda
¼ teaspoon salt
½ teaspoon ground coriander
½ teaspoon ground cinnamon
¼ cup finely chopped nuts

Preheat the oven to 350 degrees. Prepare a 6½-cup Bundt pan by lightly coating with vegetable oil cooking spray. Set aside.

Combine in a large mixing bowl the margarine and 1 cup of the sugar. Beat on high speed with an electric mixer until fluffy, 3 minutes or more. Add the egg substitute and bananas; beat until well combined. Stir in the vanilla and sour cream; continue to mix on low speed until blended smooth.

In a separate bowl, combine the flour, baking powder, soda, salt, and ground coriander. Whisk until blended. Start adding the dry mixture to the banana mixture, stirring until just mixed.

In a small mixing bowl, combine the remaining ¼ cup sugar with the cinnamon and chopped nuts. Sprinkle ⅓ of the sugar-cinnamon mixture on the bottom of the Bundt pan. Pour the batter over the sugar layer. Sprinkle the remaining nut and sugar mixture on top.

Bake for 45 minutes or until a toothpick inserted in the middle of the cake comes out clean. Let the cake stand in the pan for 5 minutes, then turn onto a rack or plate and cool completely.

APRICOT DOT CAKE

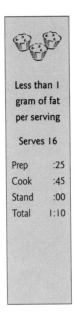

**Less than 1
gram of fat
per serving**

Serves 16

Prep	:25
Cook	:45
Stand	:00
Total	1:10

1 ⅔ cups all-purpose flour
1 teaspoon baking powder
½ teaspoon baking soda
Pinch of salt
1 (8-ounce) container fat-free cream cheese
¼ cup solid-type fat-free margarine
1 ¼ cups granulated sugar
¼ cup fat-free milk
½ cup egg substitute
¼ cup applesauce
1 teaspoon vanilla extract
1 (10-ounce) jar apricot preserves

TOPPING:

2 cups uncooked rolled oats
⅔ cup packed brown sugar
1 teaspoon ground cinnamon
⅓ cup pourable fat-free margarine

Preheat the oven to 350 degrees. Spray a 13 x 9 x 2-inch baking dish with vegetable oil cooking spray.

Combine the flour, baking powder, baking soda, and salt in a bowl and whisk to blend. Set aside.

In a large mixing bowl, combine the cream cheese, margarine, and granulated sugar. Stir gently with a wire whisk, add milk, and stir to mix. Add the egg substitute, applesauce, and vanilla. When well blended add flour mixture to cream cheese mixture, stirring carefully to blend well.

Pour half the batter into the prepared pan. Dot with the preserves and pour the remaining batter over the preserves. Bake for 35 to 40 minutes or until a toothpick inserted in the center of the cake comes out clean.

Combine topping mixture until moist and crumbly. Spread over the cake and slide under the broiler for 3 to 5 minutes or until golden brown.

CHERRY COFFEE CAKE

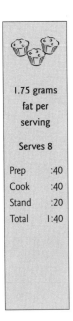

1.75 grams fat per serving

Serves 8

Prep	:40
Cook	:40
Stand	:20
Total	1:40

If using this for entertaining I would use a quiche dish — they are usually prettier than a cake pan because it is left in the baking dish until served, or I would suggest that it be cut and served on a cake platter with a pretty paper doily under the cake

TOPPING:

⅔ cup quick-cooking rolled oats

2 tablespoons all-purpose flour, rounded slightly

¼ cup packed brown sugar

2 tablespoons shredded unsweetened coconut

2 tablespoons cherry preserves or jam

CAKE:

⅓ cup evaporated skim milk

¼ cup shredded unsweetened coconut

½ cup plus 1 tablespoon drained canned cherries (see Note)

1⅓ cups all-purpose flour

⅔ cup granulated sugar

2 teaspoons baking powder

1 teaspoon baking soda

½ cup egg substitute

1 teaspoon vanilla extract

2 egg whites

GLAZE:

⅓ cup powdered sugar

1 tablespoon fat-free milk

¼ teaspoon coconut extract

1 tablespoon reserved chopped cherries

Preheat the oven to 350 degrees. Spray an 8-inch square baking dish lightly with vegetable oil cooking spray.

Prepare the topping: Combine the oats, flour, brown sugar, and coconut; toss to mix. Add the cherry preserves and toss with a fork until moistened or crumbly. Set aside.

To make the cake: In a blender, mix the skim milk and coconut; process until creamy, about 45 seconds to a minute. Transfer to a dish and set aside. Put the cherries in the blender and chop them fine; set aside.

In a medium large bowl, combine flour, sugar, baking powder, and baking soda. Blend. Add the coconut mixture, ½ cup of the chopped cherries, the egg substitute, and vanilla. Mix just enough to blend.

In a squeaky clean glass bowl, beat the egg whites until soft peaks form. Very gently fold the egg whites into the batter. Pour into the prepared baking dish; sprinkle topping evenly over the batter. Bake for 30 to 40 minutes or until a toothpick inserted in the center of the cake comes out clean. Be careful not to overbake. Cool in the pan to room temperature.

While the cake is baking, prepare the glaze: Combine the powdered sugar, milk, coconut extract, and the remaining tablespoon of chopped cherries in a bowl. Stir with a whisk until smooth. Drizzle over the cake when cooled, making swirl designs or circles.

Note: Chop the entire can of drained cherries; store excess cherries in a covered plastic container in the refrigerator. They can be added to baked goods for moisture or to sauces for meat or glazes for desserts. Use as a substitute for oil when it's called for in a muffin mix or cake mix.

BANANA BREAD

Fat-free if nuts omitted

Serves 10

Prep	:30
Cook	:45
Stand	:10
Total	1:25

1 cup sugar
3 ripe bananas, mashed
1 (6-ounce) jar puréed banana baby food
½ cup egg substitute
2 cups all-purpose flour
½ teaspoon salt (optional)
1 teaspoon baking soda
¼ cup finely chopped walnuts or pecans (optional)

Preheat the oven to 350 degrees. Prepare a 9-inch loaf pan by lightly spraying with vegetable oil cooking spray.

In the bowl of an electric mixer, combine the sugar, mashed bananas, baby food, and egg substitute. Beat on medium speed until well combined.

In another bowl, mix together the flour, salt, and baking soda.

Add the dry ingredients to the banana mixture and beat with the electric mixer until well blended. Fold in the nuts.

Pour the batter into the prepared baking dish and bake for 40 to 45 minutes or until a toothpick inserted near the center of the cake comes out clean. Cool in the pan on a wire rack for about 10 minutes. Turn out of the pan and continue to cool.

APPLE LOAF CAKE

3 to 4 apples (to yield 2½ cups chopped)
Lemon juice (optional)
I cup all-purpose flour
I teaspoon baking soda
I teaspoon ground cinnamon
½ teaspoon salt (optional)
I cup sugar
¼ cup egg substitute
½ cup fat-free margarine, melted (or ½ cup applesauce)
½ cup chopped nuts (optional)

0 grams fat if
nuts omitted

Serves 8

Prep	:35
Cook	1:00
Stand	:10
Total	1:45

Preheat the oven to 350 degrees. Lightly coat a 9-inch loaf pan with vegetable oil cooking spray.

Peel, core, and chop the apples and measure out 2½ cups. You may wish to sprinkle on a few drops of lemon juice and stir to coat the apples, to keep them from turning dark while you are preparing the cake mixture. The apples and nuts need to be added last.

Mix together the flour, baking soda, cinnamon, salt, and sugar in a mixing bowl. Blend with a wire whisk to mix evenly. Add the egg substitute and margarine or applesauce and stir to combine. The mixture will be thick. Fold in the apples and nuts. The cake will get moisture from the apples.

Bake for 60 minutes or until a cake tester inserted in the center comes out clean. Cool in the pan on a rack for 10 or 15 minutes, then turn out onto the rack to finish cooling.

PUMPKIN TEA BREAD

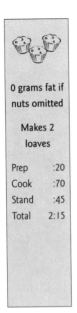

0 grams fat if nuts omitted

Makes 2 loaves

Prep	:20
Cook	:70
Stand	:45
Total	2:15

I cup applesauce
3 cups granulated sugar
¾ cup egg substitute
2 cups canned solid-pack pumpkin
2 cups all-purpose flour
½ teaspoon baking powder
½ teaspoon salt (optional)
I teaspoon baking soda
I teaspoon ground cloves
I teaspoon ground nutmeg
I teaspoon ground cinnamon
¼ cup finely chopped nuts (optional)
Whipped topping or powdered sugar glaze (optional)

Preheat the oven to 350 degrees. Prepare two 8-inch loaf pans: coat lightly with vegetable oil cooking spray and line the bottoms with waxed paper.

Combine the applesauce and sugar in a large bowl. Mix until blended, then whip in the egg substitute. Stir in the pumpkin.

In a separate bowl, combine the flour, baking powder, salt, baking soda, cloves, nutmeg, and cinnamon. Whisk until thoroughly blended. Gradually add the flour mixture to the egg mixture. When nicely blended, pour into the prepared pans. Sprinkle with the chopped nuts if desired.

Bake for 60 to 70 minutes, or until a toothpick inserted in the center of the bread comes out clean. Cool in pans for 15 minutes. Remove from pans; remove the waxed paper and finish cooling on a rack. Serve with whipped topping or glaze with a powdered sugar glaze if desired.

LEMON BREAD

1 (3-ounce) package lemon gelatin dessert mix
1 cup boiling water
1 (18¼-ounce) package reduced-fat yellow cake mix
¾ cup applesauce
1 cup egg substitute
¼ cup plus 1 teaspoon fresh lemon juice
1 teaspoon lemon zest (grated lemon rind, yellow part only)
1⅓ cups powdered sugar

0 grams fat

Serves 10

Prep	:35
Cook	:40
Stand	:10
Total	1:25

Preheat the oven to 350 degrees. Coat a 9-inch loaf pan with vegetable oil cooking spray.

In a small bowl, combine the gelatin dessert mix and the boiling water; stir to dissolve. Let cool to room temperature.

Meanwhile, put the cake mix in a large bowl. Gradually add the applesauce and egg substitute, about ¼ cup at a time, stirring to mix well. Add the cooled gelatin mixture, 1 teaspoon of the lemon juice, and the lemon zest. Continue to mix until well blended.

Pour the batter into the prepared pan and bake for 40 to 45 minutes or until a toothpick inserted in the center of the loaf comes out clean.

While the bread is baking, prepare the topping: Combine the powdered sugar with the remaining ¼ cup of lemon juice and beat until smooth. Pour and spread over the loaf when taken from the oven and before removing from the pan. Run a knife along the sides of the loaf and pull the bread slightly away from the pan to let some of the topping run down the sides. Cool in the pan.

ZUCCHINI CAKE

0 grams fat if nuts omitted

Serves 10

Prep   :45
Cook   1:00
Stand   :30
Total   2:15

¾ cup egg substitute
½ cup applesauce
⅔ cup granulated sugar
I cup packed brown sugar
I teaspoon vanilla extract
2½ cups all-purpose flour
I teaspoon baking powder
I teaspoon baking soda
I teaspoon ground nutmeg
I teaspoon ground cinnamon
2 cups shredded zucchini
I cup crushed pineapple in juice
½ cup raisins (optional)
¼ cup chopped nuts (optional)

Preheat the oven to 350 degrees. Lightly spray a 13 x 9 x 2-inch baking pan *or* two 9-inch round cake pans *or* two 9-inch loaf pans with vegetable oil cooking spray.

Combine the egg substitute, applesauce, sugars, and vanilla in the bowl of an electric mixer. Mix until smooth.

In another bowl, combine the flour, baking powder, baking soda, nutmeg, and cinnamon. Mix well. Start adding the dry ingredients to the egg mixture, a small amount at a time, mixing at low speed until all the dry ingredients are combined with the wet.

Fold in the zucchini.

Add the pineapple, and the raisins and nuts if using. Mix until just combined. Pour into the prepared pans.

Baking time will vary with choice of pans. If using loaf pans, bake for 1 hour or until a knife inserted in the center comes out clean. If using round cake pans, bake for 35 to 40 minutes, testing for doneness as with the 13 x 9-inch pan.

Cool in pan on a rack for 15 minutes, then turn out if desired and let cool completely.

HOLIDAY FRUIT BREAD

2 cups all-purpose flour
1 tablespoon baking powder
¼ teaspoon baking soda
1 teaspoon ground cinnamon
¼ teaspoon ground nutmeg
⅛ teaspoon ground ginger
1 cup sugar
1 cup canned solid-pack pumpkin
½ cup egg substitute
¼ cup applesauce
1 cup coarse-chopped fresh cranberries
½ cup chopped dried apricots

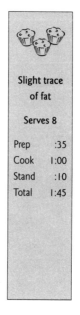

Slight trace
of fat

Serves 8

Prep	:35
Cook	1:00
Stand	:10
Total	1:45

Preheat the oven to 350 degrees. Lightly coat a 9-inch loaf pan with vegetable oil cooking spray.

Blend together the flour, baking powder, baking soda, cinnamon, nutmeg, and ginger.

In a large bowl, mix the sugar, pumpkin, egg substitute, and applesauce. When well combined, start adding the flour mixture, stirring just until moistened. Fold in the cranberries and apricots.

Pour the batter into the prepared loaf pan. Bake for about 60 to 65 minutes or until a toothpick inserted in the loaf comes out clean.

Cool in the pan for 8 to 10 minutes. Remove from the pan to a wire rack and cool completely.

MAKE-AHEAD MUFFINS

Keep a pitcher of this batter in the refrigerator for fresh hot muffins anytime you want them.

<table>
<tr><td>Less than 1 gram of fat per muffin</td></tr>
<tr><td>Makes 24</td></tr>
<tr><td>Prep</td><td>:12</td></tr>
<tr><td>Cook</td><td>:16</td></tr>
<tr><td>Stand</td><td>:02</td></tr>
<tr><td>Total</td><td>:30</td></tr>
</table>

1 cup boiling water
2 cups wheat bran
¼ cup fat-free margarine
1 cup packed brown sugar
¼ cup applesauce
2½ cups all-purpose flour
2 teaspoons baking soda
1 teaspoon ground cinnamon
¼ teaspoon salt
½ cup egg substitute
2 cups low-fat buttermilk

Add the cup of boiling water to 1 cup of wheat bran and let stand while preparing the other ingredients.

In a large bowl, cream the margarine and brown sugar together. Add the cooled wheat bran mixture and the applesauce; mix well.

In a separate container combine the flour, baking soda, cinnamon, salt, and the additional cup of wheat bran. Stir to mix thoroughly. In another bowl, whisk the egg substitute with the buttermilk.

Gradually add the flour mixture to the margarine mixture alternately with the buttermilk, beginning and ending with flour. Beat after each addition just until combined.

At this point you may either store the batter in the refrigerator in a covered container for up to a week or bake right away. Fill greased standard-size muffin tins ⅔ full and bake at 350 degrees for 16 to 18 minutes or until done to the toothpick test.

MAKE-AHEAD REFRIGERATOR MUFFINS

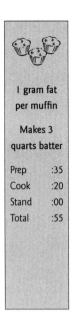

I gram fat per muffin

Makes 3 quarts batter

Prep	:35
Cook	:20
Stand	:00
Total	:55

Makes about three quarts, to be stored in the refrigerator until needed. The batter will keep up to six weeks. Great for a bake sale, with all the health-conscious people in this day and time.

5 quarts all-purpose flour
5 teaspoons baking soda
2 teaspoons salt
I (15-ounce) box raisin bran cereal
3 cups granulated sugar
I quart low-fat (I gram per cup) buttermilk
I cup egg substitute
½ cup applesauce
2 tablespoons light margarine, melted
¾ cup fat-free margarine, melted
Raisins (optional)

Mix this in a large mixing bowl. Measure the dry ingredients—flour, soda, salt, cereal, and sugar—into the container and blend thoroughly with your hands or a long-handled spoon.

Add the buttermilk, egg substitute, applesauce, and margarines. Mix thoroughly. Add additional raisins if desired. Transfer to a large wide-mouthed refrigerator jar and store in the refrigerator for up to 6 weeks.

When ready to bake, preheat the oven to 400 degrees and lightly coat muffin tins with vegetable oil cooking spray. *Without stirring,* dip out the amount of batter wanted to fill the muffin cups about ⅔ full. Bake for 20 minutes or until a toothpick inserted in one or two of the

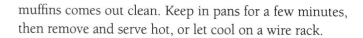

muffins comes out clean. Keep in pans for a few minutes, then remove and serve hot, or let cool on a wire rack.

Variation:

> *During the holidays you may add candied fruit when ready to bake. You may also add a few chopped nuts at the time of baking (but remember you are adding grams).*

CINNAMON ROLLS

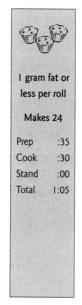

I gram fat or less per roll	
Makes 24	
Prep	:35
Cook	:30
Stand	:00
Total	1:05

4 cups self-rising flour, plus additional for coating work surface
2¼ cups fat-free evaporated milk
¾ cup fat-free margarine, at room temperature
½ stick (4 tablespoons) light margarine, at room temperature
¼ cup firmly packed brown sugar
½ cup granulated sugar
I tablespoon ground cinnamon

Preheat the oven to 375 degrees. Spray a 13 x 9 x 2-inch baking dish fairly heavily with butter-flavored cooking oil spray.

Put the flour in a mixing bowl. Add the milk ½ cup at a time, stirring just enough to blend before adding the next ½ cup. You will have a fairly heavy, sticky dough.

Turn out the dough on a heavily floured work surface and knead it very lightly with just a few turns, until it gets to a nice handling stage. Don't knead too much—the drier you get the dough, the heavier the rolls will be.

When the dough is at a workable stage, start rolling it out, making a rectangle about 12 by 24 inches, and keeping the dough about ¼ inch thick. When it is rolled out smoothly, with your fingers rub the softened margarines over to coat the dough. Mix the brown sugar and granulated sugar. Sprinkle the sugars over evenly, then sprinkle with cinnamon.

Starting with a long side, roll the dough up as for a jelly roll, ending with the seam side down. With a sharp knife dipped in flour, cut rolls about one inch thick. Transfer the rolls cut side down to the baking dish. (You may need to shape the rolls as you pick them up; sometimes they will start to unroll.) When your dish is full, spray lightly with the cooking oil spray. You may wish to sprinkle additional sugar over the top, or you may choose to sprinkle a few chopped nuts over if making a gift during the holidays. Bake for 30 to 40 minutes or until lightly browned.

Variation:

To make a tea-type cake, transfer the rolled dough to an oiled baking sheet. Split the roll several times, cutting from the center of the roll to the outside, leaving the inside of the roll attached. Spray lightly with the cooking spray. Bake for 35 to 40 minutes or until done in the center.

Cakes: Plain, Pound, Bundt, Fruited, Filled, and Layered

QUICK EASY SCRATCH CAKE

2 cups all-purpose flour
1¾ cups granulated sugar
2 teaspoons baking powder
1 teaspoon baking soda
¼ teaspoon salt
¼ cup fat-free margarine, melted
½ cup applesauce
½ cup egg substitute
¾ cup fat-free milk
1 teaspoon vanilla extract

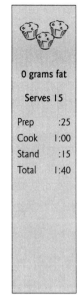

0 grams fat

Serves 15

Prep	:25
Cook	1:00
Stand	:15
Total	1:40

Preheat the oven to 350 degrees. Lightly coat a 13 x 9 x 2-inch baking pan with butter-flavored cooking oil spray.

In a large bowl, combine the flour, sugar, baking powder, baking soda, and salt. Mix well. Stir in the melted margarine and applesauce. Measure out and reserve ½ cup of this mixture.

Stir together the egg substitute, milk, and vanilla. Gradually beat into the flour and sugar mixture. Pour the batter into the prepared pan. Scatter the reserved crumbs evenly over the top.

Bake for 50 to 60 minutes or until a toothpick inserted near the center of the cake comes out clean. Let cool in the pan.

CHOCOLATE SHEET CAKE

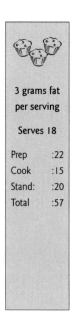

3 grams fat per serving

Serves 18

Prep	:22
Cook	:15
Stand:	:20
Total	:57

1 stick (8 tablespoons) light margarine
½ cup unsweetened cocoa powder
1 cup water
1 cup applesauce
2 cups unsifted all-purpose flour
1½ cups packed brown sugar
1 teaspoon baking soda
1 teaspoon ground cinnamon
¼ teaspoon salt (optional)
½ cup egg substitute
1 teaspoon vanilla extract
1 (14-ounce) can fat-free sweetened condensed milk (*not* evaporated milk)
1 cup powdered sugar
⅓ cup chopped nuts (optional)

Preheat the oven to 350 degrees. Lightly coat a 15½ x 10½ x 1-inch jelly roll pan with vegetable oil cooking spray.

In a small saucepan over low heat, melt 4 tablespoons of the margarine. Stir in ¼ cup of the cocoa, then the water, stirring with a small wire whisk until combined. Remove from the heat, stir in the applesauce, and set aside.

In a large mixing bowl, combine the flour, brown sugar, baking soda, cinnamon, and salt. Whisk to mix thoroughly. Add the cocoa mixture and beat well.

Combine and stir in the egg substitute, vanilla, and ⅓ cup of the condensed milk. Scrape the batter into the prepared pan and spread evenly. Bake for 15 minutes or until the cake springs back when lightly touched. Cool for 20 minutes while you prepare the icing.

Icing: In the same small saucepan, melt the remaining 4 tablespoons of margarine. Stir in the remaining ¼ cup of cocoa and the remaining condensed milk. Add the powdered sugar and stir until smooth and creamy. Spread on the warm (not hot) cake. Sprinkle with chopped nuts if desired. To serve, cut into squares; serve with fat-free vanilla ice cream or frozen yogurt.

SPICED SNACK CAKE

Excellent with Apple Cider Sauce, page 113.

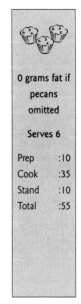

0 grams fat if	
pecans	
omitted	
Serves 6	
Prep	:10
Cook	:35
Stand	:10
Total	:55

1 ⅔ cups all-purpose flour
1 cup packed brown sugar
1 ½ teaspoons ground allspice
1 teaspoon baking soda
½ teaspoon salt (optional)
¾ cup applesauce
½ cup water
1 teaspoon apple cider vinegar
⅓ cup chopped pecans (optional)

Preheat the oven to 350 degrees. Have ready an ungreased 8-inch square baking pan.

In a large bowl, combine the flour, brown sugar, allspice, baking soda, and salt. With a wire whisk, blend all these ingredients well. Mix in the applesauce, water, vinegar, and pecans if desired.

Mix well. Pour into the prepared pan and bake for 35 to 40 minutes or until a toothpick inserted in the center comes out clean. Let stand for 10 minutes before cutting.

OATMEAL CAKE

A very moist cake, this freezes well and is a great make-ahead cake, actually better the second day.

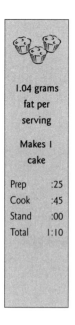

1.04 grams
fat per
serving

Makes 1
cake

Prep   :25
Cook   :45
Stand   :00
Total   1:10

1 cup quick-cooking rolled oats
1½ cups boiling water
1 cup packed brown sugar
1 cup granulated sugar
½ cup egg substitute
½ cup solid-type fat-free margarine, at room temperature
1½ cups all-purpose flour
1 teaspoon baking soda
1 teaspoon ground cinnamon
Pinch of salt

TOPPING:

½ cup shredded sweetened dried coconut
½ cup solid-type fat-free margarine, melted
1 cup packed brown sugar
¼ cup fat-free sweetened condensed milk (*not* evaporated milk)
1 teaspoon vanilla extract
¼ cup chopped nuts (optional)

Preheat the oven to 350 degrees. Lightly coat a 13 x 9 x 2-inch baking pan with vegetable oil cooking spray.

Combine the oats and boiling water in a small bowl and set aside until needed.

In a mixing bowl, combine the brown and white sugars with the egg substitute and margarine. Stir until well blended.

In another bowl, whisk together the flour, baking soda, cinnamon, and salt. Add to the sugar mixture and stir to blend thoroughly. Stir in the oats until evenly mixed. Pour into the prepared pan and bake about 40 minutes or until the cake springs back when lightly touched.

Prepare the topping: Mix together the coconut, nuts, melted margarine, brown sugar, condensed milk, and vanilla. Spread over the warm cake and slide under the broiler until brown and bubbly. Watch closely—different broilers cook differently at different levels, and you don't want this to burn.

HONEY OATMEAL CAKE

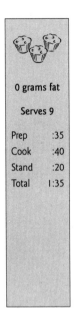

0 grams fat

Serves 9

Prep   :35
Cook   :40
Stand   :20
Total   1:35

Excellent served warm, as a breakfast cake or with a caramel sauce or caramel frosting.

1 cup regular or quick-cooking rolled oats
½ cup solid-type fat-free margarine
1¼ cups boiling water
1½ cups honey
1 teaspoon vanilla extract
½ cup egg substitute
1¾ cups sifted whole wheat flour
1 teaspoon baking soda
¾ teaspoon salt (optional)
1 teaspoon ground cinnamon
¼ teaspoon ground nutmeg

Preheat the oven to 350 degrees. Lightly coat an 11 x 7 x 1½-inch baking pan with vegetable oil cooking spray.

In a large mixing bowl, combine the oats, margarine, and boiling water. Let stand for 20 minutes.

Add to the oat mixture the honey, vanilla, and egg substitute. Stir until mixed well. Whisk together the flour, baking soda, salt, cinnamon, and nutmeg. Add the dry ingredients to the oat mixture; stir until thoroughly mixed. Pour into the prepared pan and bake for 30 to 40 minutes or until a cake tester or toothpick inserted in the center comes out clean.

CRAZY CAKE

Serve with fat-free frozen yogurt or ice cream or frozen whipped topping thawed.

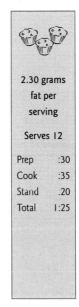

2.30 grams
fat per
serving

Serves 12

Prep   :30
Cook   :35
Stand   :20
Total   1:25

1 (18¼-ounce) box reduced-fat light yellow cake mix
¼ cup light margarine
¼ cup fat-free margarine
¾ cup egg substitute
1 (8-ounce) package fat-free cream cheese, at room temperature
1 (16-ounce) package powdered sugar
1 teaspoon vanilla extract
½ cup chopped pecans (optional)

Preheat the oven to 350 degrees. Lightly coat a 13 x 9 x 2-inch baking pan with vegetable oil cooking spray.

Empty the cake mix into a large bowl and add both margarines and ¼ cup of the egg substitute. Stir until crumbly and well mixed. Pat the mixture into the prepared baking pan.

Using the same bowl, combine and mix well the cream cheese, the remaining ½ cup of the egg substitute, the powdered sugar, and the vanilla. Pour over the cake mixture; sprinkle with the pecans.

Bake for 35 minutes or until nicely browned. Cool in the pan on a rack. To serve, cut into squares.

CARROT CAKE

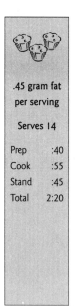

**.45 gram fat
per serving**

Serves 14

Prep	:40
Cook	:55
Stand	:45
Total	2:20

As far back as I can remember there has always been carrot cake. I have a healthy carrot cake recipe to keep the tradition going. Can you remember a time without carrot cakes? Not only are they good — they are good for you. Each serving is a great source of vitamin A.

8 to 10 fresh carrots (about 1½ pounds) (4 cups grated used in recipe)
2¾ cups all-purpose flour
1⅓ cups sugar
2 teaspoons baking soda
1 teaspoon ground cinnamon, or more to taste
1 cup orange juice
1 cup egg substitute
2 teaspoons vanilla extract
½ cup raisins (optional)
¼ cup ground nuts (optional—will add fat grams to your cake)

Preheat the oven to 350 degrees. Spray a 13 x 9 x 2-inch baking pan lightly with vegetable oil cooking spray.

Grate the carrots, using the grating attachment of your food processor, and measure out 4 cups for this recipe. Set aside.

Combine in a large mixing bowl the flour, sugar, soda, and cinnamon. Stir with a wire whisk to blend.

Add the orange juice, egg substitute, and vanilla. Continue to stir by hand, or you may use an electric mixer at this point. Fold in the carrots and raisins and nuts if using. Pour the batter into the prepared pan and spread evenly.

Bake for 55 to 60 minutes or until a toothpick inserted near the center comes out clean. Cool in the pan on a rack. When cool, frost with cream cheese frosting (pages 104 and 105).

PUMPKIN PIE CAKE

Great holiday cake and pie all in one. Serve with fat-free vanilla ice cream or frozen yogurt.

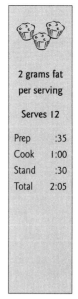

2 grams fat
per serving

Serves 12

Prep	:35
Cook	1:00
Stand	:30
Total	2:05

1 large (30-ounce) can pumpkin pie mix or filling
1 (18¼-ounce) package reduced-fat yellow cake mix
½ cup pourable fat-free margarine
¼ cup finely chopped pecans (optional)

Preheat the oven to 350 degrees. Lightly spray a 13 x 9 x 2-inch baking pan with vegetable oil cooking spray.

Prepare the pumpkin according to package directions for making a pie. Transfer to the prepared baking pan.

Sprinkle the dry cake mix evenly over the pumpkin mixture. Pour margarine on top and sprinkle evenly with the nuts.

Bake for 30 minutes. Remove from the oven. With the handle of a wooden spoon, poke holes in the cake at random. Return to the oven and bake an additional 30 minutes. Let the cake cool in the pan on a rack.

PUMPKIN PUFF CAKE

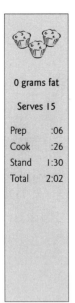

0 grams fat

Serves 15

Prep	:06
Cook	:26
Stand	1:30
Total	2:02

1 (30-ounce) can pumpkin pie filling
1 (16-ounce) package angel food cake mix

TOPPING:

¾ cup fat-free sweetened condensed milk (*not* evaporated milk)
1 cup canned solid-pack pumpkin
2 cups powdered sugar
2 tablespoons nonfat vanilla instant pudding
2 cups fat-free whipped topping, thawed

Preheat the oven to 375 degrees. Lightly spray the bottom of a 13 x 9 x 2-inch baking pan with vegetable oil cooking spray.

Empty the can of pumpkin pie filling into a mixing bowl. Pour the cake mix over and blend with a wire whisk until thoroughly moist and smooth.

Pour into the prepared pan and bake for 28 to 30 minutes. Remove from the oven; let stand until cool, about 1 hour.

Meanwhile, combine your topping:

Mix the condensed milk, solid-pack pumpkin, powdered sugar, and vanilla pudding mix. Blend for 3 or 4 minutes. Refrigerate for 25 or 30 minutes. Fold in the whipped topping.

Cover the cooled cake with the prepared topping. Keep refrigerated until time to serve, and refrigerate any leftover cake.

LEMANGEL DELIGHT

1 (16-ounce) package angel food cake mix
1 (16-ounce) can lemon pie filling

GLAZE:

½ cup powdered sugar
1 tablespoon lemon juice

0 grams fat		
Serves 15		
Prep		:06
Cook		:26
Stand		1:00
Total		1:32

Preheat the oven to 375 degrees. Lightly spray a 13 x 9 x 2-inch pan with vegetable oil cooking spray.

Combine the cake mix and pie filling in a bowl. Blend with a wire whisk or electric mixer on medium speed. When well blended, pour into the prepared pan. Bake for 26 minutes.

Remove from the oven and let cool to room temperature, about 1 hour.

Prepare the glaze: In a small bowl, mix the powdered sugar with the lemon juice. Using a small wire whisk, stir until smooth. Set aside.

When the cake is cool, drizzle the glaze over all. If serving for a special occasion you may like to use a bunch of fresh mint. Garnish each piece with one fresh mint leaf in the center.

WACKY CAKE

**1.5 grams fat
entire cake**

Serves 4

Prep	:15
Cook	:35
Stand	:10
Total	1:00

1½ cups all-purpose flour
1 cup sugar
3 tablespoons unsweetened cocoa powder
½ teaspoon baking soda
½ teaspoon salt
1 tablespoon vinegar
5 tablespoons applesauce
1 teaspoon vanilla extract
1 cup water

Preheat the oven to 350 degrees. Cut a square of waxed paper to fit the bottom of an 8-inch square baking pan, and line the pan.

Mix together in the pan the flour, sugar, cocoa, baking soda, and salt. With the back of a spoon make three holes in the dry mixture.

To the first hole add 1 tablespoon of vinegar.

To the second hole add 5 tablespoons of applesauce.

To the third hole add 1 teaspoon of vanilla.

Pour the water over all. Mix until well blended and smooth. Bake for 30 to 35 minutes or until the cake springs back to the touch.

Cool in the pan on a wire rack and add your favorite frosting or sauce, or serve plain with coffee.

BROWNIE SHEET CAKE

1 cup water
1½ cups solid-type fat-free margarine
½ cup unsweetened cocoa powder
2 cups granulated sugar
2 cups all-purpose flour
1 teaspoon baking soda
1 teaspoon ground cinnamon
½ cup egg substitute
½ cup low-fat buttermilk (1 gram per cup) plus ⅓ cup additional for
    frosting
1 (16-ounce) box powdered sugar
⅓ cup chopped nuts (optional)

.32 gram fat
per serving

Serves 15

Prep   :25
Cook   :20
Stand   :50
Total   1:35

Preheat the oven to 400 degrees. Coat a 15½ x 10½ x 1-inch jelly roll pan with vegetable oil cooking spray.

In a large heavy saucepan combine the water, 1 cup margarine, and ¼ cup of the cocoa. Stir over medium heat with a wire whisk to blend. When the margarine is melted, stir in the sugar.

Mix together in a separate bowl the flour, baking soda, and cinnamon. Stir into the margarine mixture. Add the egg substitute, then ½ cup buttermilk. Mix well.

Pour into the prepared pan and spread to smooth the surface. Bake for about 20 minutes or until done to the touch.

While the cake is baking, make the frosting. It needs to be poured over the cake while hot.

Heat ⅓ cup of buttermilk and the remaining ½ cup margarine together in a heavy saucepan over low heat, stirring to mix well. When the mixture comes to a boil, remove from the heat and pour over the powdered sugar and the remaining ¼ cup of cocoa, which have been blended together in a separate bowl. Mix with a wire whisk or electric mixer until smooth. Fold in the nuts if desired. Pour over the cake while hot and spread with a spatula to cover the surface.

Cool in the pan on a rack. Cut into squares to serve.

POUND CAKE

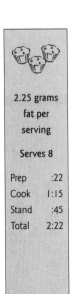

2.25 grams
fat per
serving

Serves 8

Prep   :22
Cook   1:15
Stand   :45
Total   2:22

½ stick (4 tablespoons) reduced-fat margarine
¼ cup solid-type or tub fat-free margarine
1 cup sugar
1 cup egg substitute
2 cups all-purpose flour
1 teaspoon baking powder
Dash of salt
1 teaspoon vanilla extract
½ teaspoon almond extract

Preheat the oven to 350 degrees. Lightly spray the sides and bottom of a 9 x 5 x 3-inch loaf pan with vegetable oil cooking spray. Line the bottom of the pan with waxed paper and spray the waxed paper.

In the bowl of an electric mixer, beat the two margarines together until light, then gradually beat in the sugar. Continue beating for about 3 minutes or until fluffy. Gradually add the egg substitute, beating well after each addition.

In a separate bowl, whisk together the flour, baking powder, and salt. Blend into the egg mixture gradually, then mix in the vanilla and almond extracts and beat just until smooth.

Pour the batter into the prepared loaf pan. Bake for 1 hour and 15 minutes. Let cool in the pan for 30 minutes. Carefully turn out of the pan, remove the waxed paper, turn the cake right side up, and let finish cooling on a rack.

Variation:

> *To make lemon pound cake, omit the vanilla and almond extracts. Add 1 teaspoon of lemon flavoring.*

APPLE POUND CAKE

4 grams fat
per serving

Serves 12

Prep	:45
Cook	1:20
Stand	:25
Total	2:30

1 stick (8 tablespoons) light margarine (6 grams per tablespoon), at room temperature
2 cups granulated sugar
¾ cup egg substitute
1 cup applesauce
1 tablespoon vanilla extract
3 cups all-purpose flour
1 teaspoon baking soda
1 teaspoon salt
3 cups diced peeled apples
2 tablespoons low-fat shredded coconut
½ cup chopped nuts (optional)

Preheat the oven to 350 degrees. Lightly coat a 10 x 3¾-inch fluted tube or Bundt pan with vegetable oil cooking spray. Sprinkle the oiled pan with flour, turning to make sure it is completely coated, then turn upside down and tap out the excess.

In the bowl of an electric mixer, beat the margarine until light, then gradually add the sugar and continue beating for about 3 minutes or until fluffy. Gradually add the egg substitute, beating well after each addition. Stir in the applesauce and vanilla just until blended.

In a separate bowl, whisk together the flour, baking soda, and salt. Start adding to the applesauce mixture, about ¼ at a time, mixing well after each addition.

Fold in the apples, coconut, and chopped nuts. Pour and scrape into the prepared pan and bake for 1 hour and 20 minutes or until a wooden toothpick inserted in the center comes out clean.

Let the cake cool in the pan for about 15 minutes. Carefully turn out of the pan and finish cooling on a rack.

Store the cake at room temperature wrapped in foil; it will keep for several days. It freezes well.

LEMON POUND CAKE

1 cup egg substitute
1 (18¼-ounce) reduced-fat yellow cake mix
1 (4-ounce) package instant lemon pudding mix
¾ cup water
½ cup applesauce

GLAZE:

⅓ cup lemon juice
2 cups powdered sugar
Thinly sliced lemon (optional)

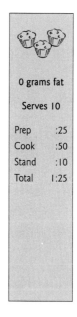

0 grams fat

Serves 10

Prep	:25
Cook	:50
Stand	:10
Total	1:25

Preheat the oven to 350 degrees. Prepare a 10-inch tube cake pan with removable bottom. Spray the bottom lightly with vegetable oil cooking spray, dust with flour very lightly, and tap off the excess flour.

In a medium-size mixing bowl, with an electric mixer, beat the egg substitute until lemon-colored. Add the cake mix, the dry pudding mix, water, and applesauce. Beat until well blended.

Pour the mixture into the prepared cake pan. Bake for 50 minutes.

While cake stands for about 10 minutes in the oven, make the glaze: Combine the lemon juice and powdered sugar in a saucepan, stirring with a wire whisk until blended. Heat to boiling, stirring all the time.

Remove the cake from the oven and run a knife around the inside to release the tube ring, leaving the cake on the pan bottom. Using a two-pronged carving fork, punch holes all over the cake. Drizzle the glaze over the top and spread on the sides. Let cool on a rack.

To serve, place on a pretty serving plate and garnish with twisted lemon slices if desired.

BUNDT CAKE

4 grams fat
per serving

Serves 14

Prep   :26
Cook   1:10
Stand   :15
Total   1:51

¼ cup (4 tablespoons) reduced-fat margarine
¼ cup solid-type fat-free margarine
¾ cup packed brown sugar
¾ cup egg substitute
¾ cup water
I teaspoon vanilla extract
2½ cups all-purpose flour
¼ cup buttermilk powder
I teaspoon baking powder
I teaspoon baking soda
I teaspoon ground cinnamon
½ cup apricot or peach jam or orange marmalade

Preheat the oven to 350 degrees. Lightly but thoroughly coat the inside of an 8¼ x 3¼-inch Bundt or fluted tube pan with vegetable oil cooking spray. Dust with flour and turn the pan from side to side to make sure it is completely coated. Invert the pan and tap out excess flour.

In the bowl of an electric mixer, combine the two margarines and beat until light. Gradually add the brown sugar and continue to beat for about 3 minutes or until fluffy.

Mix the egg substitute, the water, and the vanilla; gradually add to the margarine-sugar mixture, stirring until well blended.

In a separate bowl, whisk together the flour, buttermilk powder, baking powder, baking soda, and cinnamon. Stir into the margarine-sugar mixture until thoroughly blended. Fold in the jam.

Pour and scrape the batter into the prepared pan and bake for 60 to 70 minutes or until the cake springs back when lightly pressed. Cool in the pan for 15 minutes, then invert onto a wire rack and remove from the pan.

GERMAN APPLE CAKE

Less than 1 gram fat per serving

Serves 10

Prep :35
Cook 1:30
Stand :10
Total 2:15

This used to be Mom's favorite recipe to send with her grandson on his hunting trips. The other men loved it also. The only difference is that Mom made the fat-full recipe and I make the fat-free recipe. This is a great make-ahead cake that keeps up to a week and also freezes well.

4 to 5 baking or cooking apples such as Granny Smith
2 cups plus 5 tablespoons granulated sugar
2 teaspoons ground cinnamon
3 cups all-purpose flour
1¼ teaspoons salt (optional)
1½ teaspoons baking soda
1½ teaspoons baking powder
1 cup egg substitute
1 cup applesauce
2 teaspoons vanilla extract
⅓ cup orange juice

GLAZE:

1½ cups powdered sugar
2 tablespoons solid-type or pourable fat-free margarine
1 to 2 tablespoons water

Preheat the oven to 350 degrees. Spray an 8¼ x 3¼-inch fluted tube or Bundt pan with vegetable oil cooking oil spray. Dust with flour while rotating the pan so that all surfaces are completely coated. Tap out excess flour; set aside.

Peel, core, and thinly slice the apples into a bowl. Combine 5 tablespoons of the sugar with the cinnamon; sprinkle over the apples and toss to cover them evenly. Set aside.

In a large mixing bowl combine the flour, the remaining 2 cups sugar, and the salt, soda, and baking powder. Whisk to blend evenly. Add the egg substitute, applesauce, vanilla, and orange juice. With an electric mixer, blend on low speed for 1 minute; increase speed and blend an additional 3 minutes.

Fill the prepared pan with alternating layers of batter, then of apples, then batter, then apples, and finally batter, ending with a few apple slices on top. Arranging the apples in a circle of half-moon slices makes a nice presentation.

Bake for 1 hour and 30 minutes or until a tester inserted in the center of the cake comes out clean. Remove to a wire rack for 10 minutes, then invert to remove from the pan and continue to cool.

Meanwhile, prepare the glaze: Mix the powdered sugar, margarine, and water until smooth. Drizzle on the cooled cake.

TUNNEL OF FRUIT CAKE

Less than ½ gram fat per serving

Serves 14

Prep	:35
Cook	:55
Stand	:25
Total	1:55

1 (18¼-ounce) package reduced-fat yellow cake mix, ¼ cup reserved
3 tablespoons applesauce
1 tablespoon pure maple syrup
¾ cup egg substitute
⅔ cup water
3 tablespoons frozen apple juice concentrate, thawed
1 (20-ounce) can fruit pie filling, such as apple, divided in half
¼ cup packed brown sugar
¼ cup quick-cooking rolled oats
Apple Cider Sauce or Rum Sauce for Cakes or Desserts (both on page 113)

Preheat the oven to 350 degrees. Lightly coat a 10-inch tube pan with removable bottom with vegetable oil cooking spray, dust with flour until thoroughly and evenly coated, and tap out excess. Set aside.

In a large bowl, combine the cake mix (don't forget to reserve ¼ cup), applesauce, maple syrup, egg substitute, water, and apple juice concentrate. With an electric mixer, beat on low speed for 1 minute, then turn to high and continue to mix for 2 more minutes until smooth and well blended.

Pour half the batter into the prepared pan. With your fingers or tongs, pick up single pieces of fruit from the pie filling and arrange in a circle over the batter, beginning in the middle—the fruit should not touch the edges. Use just about half the can, reserving the rest for the sauce. Pour and scrape the remaining batter over the fruit; spread to smooth out nicely.

Combine the reserved ¼ cup of cake mix with the brown sugar and oats. Sprinkle evenly over the top of the cake batter. Bake for 55 to 60 minutes or until a wooden pick inserted in the center of the cake comes out clean. Cool in the pan on a rack for 25 to 30 minutes; run a knife around the inside to release the tube ring, leaving the cake on the pan bottom.

Prepare apple rum sauce, using the remaining half can of fruit. Pour over the top and let it drizzle down the sides of the cake.

PEACH BRANDY CAKE

1 (18¼-ounce) package reduced-fat yellow cake mix
½ cup egg substitute
1 (8-ounce) container peach yogurt
1 (21-ounce) can sliced peaches, juice and all
2 tablespoons peach brandy

GLAZE:

½ cup peach preserves
2 tablespoons peach brandy

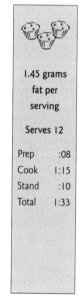

1.45 grams
fat per
serving

Serves 12

Prep	:08
Cook	1:15
Stand	:10
Total	1:33

Preheat the oven to 375 degrees. Lightly coat a 10 x 3¾-inch fluted tube or Bundt pan with vegetable oil cooking spray. Sprinkle in 1 or 2 tablespoons of flour, turning and tapping the pan to make sure it is thoroughly and evenly coated. Knock out excess flour.

Combine the cake mix, egg substitute, and yogurt in the bowl of an electric mixer. Mix on low speed until moist. Add the canned peaches with their juice and the brandy.

Continue to mix at medium speed for 1 minute. Turn to higher speed and beat 2 additional minutes until very well mixed and the peaches are chopped.

Pour the batter into the prepared pan and bake for 55 to 60 minutes. Begin checking for doneness after 50 minutes with a wooden toothpick; the cake is done when no crumbs adhere to the pick.

Let the cake cool in the pan on a rack for 10 minutes. Cover the pan with a serving plate and carefully invert to turn the cake out.

While the cake continues to cool, make the glaze: Put the preserves and brandy in a small saucepan and bring to a boil over low heat. Let simmer 1 minute while you watch and stir carefully. Pour the glaze over the warm cake, letting it drizzle down the sides. Cut after cooled completely.

APRICOT NECTAR CAKE

1 (18¼-ounce) package reduced-fat yellow cake mix
1 (3-ounce) box lemon Jell-0
1 cup egg substitute
¾ cup apricot nectar
½ cup applesauce
2 tablespoons vegetable oil
1 teaspoon lemon flavoring

GLAZE:

1 cup powdered sugar
Juice of 1 lemon

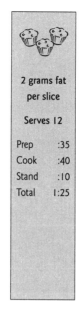

2 grams fat
per slice

Serves 12

Prep	:35
Cook	:40
Stand	:10
Total	1:25

Preheat the oven to 350 degrees. Lightly coat a 10 x 3¾-inch fluted tube or Bundt pan with vegetable oil cooking spray. Sprinkle in 1 or 2 tablespoons of flour, turning and tapping the pan to make sure it is thoroughly and evenly coated. Knock out excess flour.

In a large bowl combine the cake mix, dry Jell-O, egg substitute, apricot nectar, applesauce, oil, and lemon flavoring. Mix at medium speed until well blended.

Pour into the prepared pan and bake for 35 to 40 minutes or until a wooden pick inserted in the center of the cake comes out clean.

Let the cake cool in the pan on a rack for 10 minutes. Cover with a plate and invert carefully to turn the cake out. While the cake is still hot, punch holes in the surface with an ice pick or carving fork.

Make the glaze: Mix the powdered sugar and lemon juice, stirring with a wire whisk until smooth. Pour over the warm cake and let it drizzle down the sides. Spread with a spatula to cover evenly. Allow the cake to cool before cutting.

CARAMEL APRICOT CAKE

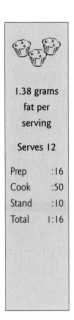

Just wait until the preacher gets a bite of this one!

1.38 grams fat per serving

Serves 12

Prep	:16
Cook	:50
Stand	:10
Total	1:16

1 (18¼-ounce) reduced-fat caramel flavored cake mix
1 (3-ounce) package instant butterscotch pudding mix
2 tablespoons apricot brandy
½ cup water
½ cup egg substitute
1 (6-ounce) jar apricot with tapioca baby food

TOPPING:

½ cup nutlike cereal
½ cup packed brown sugar
4 tablespoons apricot brandy
2 teaspoons lower-in-fat shredded coconut
1 (14-ounce) can fat-free sweetened condensed milk
   (*not* evaporated milk)

Preheat the oven to 375 degrees. Lightly coat a 10 x 3¾-inch Bundt or fluted tube pan with vegetable oil cooking spray. Dust with flour until the pan is thoroughly and evenly coated; knock out excess. Set aside.

In the bowl of an electric mixer, combine the dry cake mix with the pudding mix; stir to blend. Add the 2 tablespoons brandy, ½ cup water, the egg substitute, and the baby food. Mix at medium speed until well blended and smooth.

Make the topping: In a separate small bowl, combine the cereal, brown sugar, 2 tablespoons of the brandy, and the coconut. Mix with your hands or a fork until crumbly.

Distribute the topping in small amounts on the bottom and partly up the sides of the prepared pan. When covered as evenly as possible, carefully pour the batter in. Bake for 45 to 50 minutes or until a wooden pick inserted in the center of the cake comes out clean.

Remove the cake from the oven and let it cool in the pan for at least 10 minutes before inverting it carefully on a serving plate. If any topping sticks to the pan, scrape it off and replace it on the cake. Be sure to get it all—it is the best part.

In a small saucepan, combine the condensed milk and the remaining 2 tablespoons brandy. Bring to a very low simmer for 1 minute; remove from the heat and pour over the cake.

CHOCOLATE CHERRY SUPREME

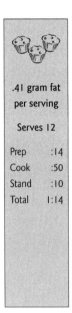

.41 gram fat
per serving

Serves 12

Prep	:14
Cook	:50
Stand	:10
Total	1:14

1 (18¼-ounce) reduced-fat chocolate cake mix
½ cup egg substitute
1 (16-ounce) can tart cherries in water, undrained
4 tablespoons cherry wine
2 cups cherry preserves

Preheat the oven to 375 degrees. Lightly coat a 10 x 3¾-inch Bundt or fluted tube pan with vegetable oil cooking spray. Dust with flour to coat evenly; knock out excess flour. Set aside.

In the bowl of an electric mixer, combine the dry cake mix with the egg substitute and the undrained can of cherries. Mix slowly to combine. When all is moist, increase the speed to medium high and beat for at least 2 minutes. The mixer will crush the cherries until small pieces. Stir in 2 tablespoons of the wine.

Pour ¾ of the batter into the prepared pan. Spoon 1 cup of the preserves in a circle around the center of the batter. (This will form a tunnel effect when baked.) Pour and scrape the remaining batter over the preserves. Bake for 45 to 55 minutes or until a wooden pick inserted in the center of the cake comes out clean.

Cool the cake in the pan for at least 10 minutes. Meanwhile, prepare the glaze: In a small saucepan, combine the remaining cup of preserves with the remaining 2 tablespoons of wine. Bring to a low simmer and continue to simmer for 1 minute; remove from the heat.

Place a serving plate over the top of the cake pan and carefully invert the cake. Remove the pan and pour the hot glaze, a small amount at a time, over the top of the cake, letting it drizzle down the sides. Guide with a spoon to ensure that the cake is coated evenly. Let cool before cutting.

PINEAPPLE UPSIDE-DOWN CAKE

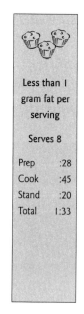

I can remember this was one of the cakes that Mom could afford to make when we were little. She used a cast iron skillet, I remember seeing her put about 3/4 cup of pure butter in that skillet and melting it. I can just almost smell the aroma now. I am afraid that I make mine quite differently, but you know what? I think it is every bit as good as the cake she made, and a lot healthier. I always enjoy flipping the cake and seeing how pretty it is and how well it came out of the pan.

Less than I gram fat per serving

Serves 8

Prep	:28
Cook	:45
Stand	:20
Total	1:33

2 tablespoons solid-type low-fat margarine (4.5 grams per table-spoon)
I cup packed brown sugar
I (20-ounce) can sliced pineapple, drained
24 maraschino cherries, drained
I (18¼-ounce) package reduced-fat yellow cake mix
I cup water
¾ cup egg substitute

Preheat the oven to 350 degrees. Spray a heavy 10-inch skillet (with ovenproof handle) or a 9-inch square baking pan fairly heavily with butter-flavored cooking spray.

Put the margarine in the skillet and place in the oven for a few minutes until the margarine is melted. Sprinkle the brown sugar evenly over the bottom of the pan and pat gently to fill any holes. Arrange the pineapple slices in a pattern on the sugar, touching but not overlapping. Some may go up the sides of the pan just a little but that is OK. Place a couple of cherries in each pineapple center, or fill the spaces with cherries if desired.

In a mixing bowl combine the dry cake mix with the water and egg substitute. Beat until well blended and smooth. Pour and scrape over the prepared topping.

Bake for 40 to 45 minutes or until a wooden pick inserted in the center of the cake comes out clean. Remove from the oven and let stand for 15 to 20 minutes. Loosen the edges of the cake. Place a heatproof serving dish upside down on top of the pan. Flip the pan and dish over together; leave the pan over the cake for 1 or 2 minutes, then carefully lift the pan straight up. Serve the cake warm or cold.

PINEAPPLE BAR CAKE

1½ cups all-purpose flour
1 teaspoon baking powder
¼ teaspoon baking soda
Pinch of salt
½ cup applesauce
2 tablespoons fat-free margarine, at room temperature
2 cups sugar
1 cup egg substitute
1 (14-ounce) can crushed pineapple, drained
¼ cup chopped pecans (optional)

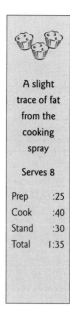

A slight
trace of fat
from the
cooking
spray

Serves 8

Prep	:25
Cook	:40
Stand	:30
Total	1:35

Preheat the oven to 350 degrees. Lightly coat an 8- or 9-inch loaf pan with vegetable oil cooking spray. Dust with flour and tap out excess.

In a small bowl, combine the flour, baking powder, baking soda, and salt. Set aside.

In a large mixing bowl, combine the applesauce, margarine, and sugar; mix well to blend. Beat in the egg substitute ¼ cup at a time. Gradually beat in the flour alternately with the pineapple, beginning and ending with flour.

Pour and scrape the batter into the prepared pan. Sprinkle with nuts if desired. Bake for 30 to 40 minutes or until a wooden pick inserted in the center comes out clean.

Remove from the oven and let cool in the pan for 15 minutes. Loosen the edges of the cake if necessary. Invert onto a rack, turn right side up, and let finish cooling on the rack. To serve, cut into slices (or bars).

"THE BEST CAKE"

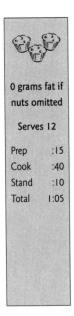

0 grams fat if nuts omitted

Serves 12

Prep	:15
Cook	:40
Stand	:10
Total	1:05

This cake recipe was in my first, self-published cookbook, and it appeared in my first book when nationally published. It has been my number-one all-time bestseller. I just could not risk the fact that some of you may not have my first book and would never know this cake. It is great. It is so easy it is embarrassing. I hope that you will enjoy this cake half as much as I have.

½ cup egg substitute
2 cups granulated sugar
2 cups all-purpose flour
2 teaspoons baking soda
1 (20-ounce) can crushed pineapple, juice and all (2½ cups)
1 teaspoon vanilla extract
¼ cup chopped nuts (optional)

FROSTING

1 (8-ounce) package fat-free cream cheese, softened
1½ cups powdered sugar
¼ teaspoon vanilla extract

Preheat the oven to 350 degrees. Spray a 13 x 9 x 2-inch pan with vegetable oil cooking spray.

In a medium large mixing bowl, beat the egg substitute and granulated sugar together with an electric mixer. Mix the flour and the baking soda; beat into the egg substitute mixture. Add the pineapple and continue to beat with the mixer. This will crush the pineapple slightly. When well blended, stir in the vanilla and nuts if using.

Pour into the prepared pan, scraping the sides of the bowl. You don't want to miss a bite of this one. Bake for 35 to 40 minutes, until a wooden pick inserted in the center of the cake comes out clean.

Meanwhile, mix the frosting ingredients: Stir the cream cheese with a wire whisk, not the mixer. (Fat-free cream cheese has a water base and gets runny easily.) Gradually add the powdered sugar, then stir in the vanilla. If the frosting is runny, don't be alarmed. Use it anyway if you have left your cake in a pan. If making a layer cake, add just a tiny bit of instant vanilla pudding, about 1 teaspoon at a time, until you have the consistency desired.

Let the cake cool about 10 minutes and frost. Sprinkle with additional nuts if desired.

YUMMY CAKE

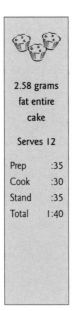

2.58 grams
fat entire
cake

Serves 12

Prep	:35
Cook	:30
Stand	:35
Total	1:40

1½ cups all-purpose flour
⅓ cup chopped dates
1 cup sugar
½ cup applesauce
¼ cup egg substitute
1 cup low-fat buttermilk (1 gram per cup)
2 tablespoons unsweetened cocoa powder
1 teaspoon vinegar
1 teaspoon baking soda
Pinch of salt (optional)
1 teaspoon vanilla extract
¼ cup chopped pecans (optional)

ICING

1 (20-ounce) can crushed pineapple, juice and all

Preheat the oven to 350 degrees. Lightly coat a 13 x 9 x 2-inch baking pan with vegetable oil cooking spray.

Measure the flour into a bowl. Add the chopped dates and toss to dredge. Set aside.

In the large bowl of an electric mixer, combine the sugar, applesauce, and egg substitute. Beat until well mixed.

In a separate small bowl, combine the buttermilk, cocoa, vinegar, soda, salt, and vanilla.

Add the flour-date mixture and the buttermilk to the applesauce mixture, beginning and ending with flour. Beat well after each addition. Stir in the pecans if using.

Pour and scrape into the prepared pan. Bake for 25 to 30 minutes or until a wooden pick inserted in the center of the cake comes out clean. Remove from the oven and cool in the pan on a rack.

Meanwhile, make the icing: Combine the pineapple and its juices with the sugar in a saucepan. Cook, stirring often, over low heat until the mixture is thick and almost candylike. Remove from the heat.

When the icing is cool, spread it over the cooled cake. To serve, cut into squares.

DUTCH APPLE CAKE

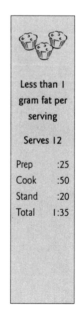

Less than 1 gram fat per serving

Serves 12

Prep	:25
Cook	:50
Stand	:20
Total	1:35

¾ cup pourable fat-free margarine
¾ cup quick-cooking rolled oats
¾ cup packed brown sugar
1 tablespoon all-purpose flour
¼ cup chopped nuts (optional)
1 (18¼-ounce) package reduced-fat white or yellow cake mix
¾ cup water
¾ cup egg substitute
2 (21-ounce) cans apple pie filling or fruit pie filling of your choice
½ teaspoon ground cinnamon

Preheat the oven to 350 degrees. Pour ½ cup of the margarine over the bottom of a 13 x 9 x 2-inch baking pan. With a spatula, spread it evenly over the surface.

In a small mixing bowl, combine the oats, brown sugar, flour, and nuts if using. Pour in the remaining ¼ cup of margarine. Mix well until moist and crumbly. Set aside.

In a separate mixing bowl, combine the cake mix, water, and egg substitute. With a wire whisk or electric mixer, beat until well blended. Pour into the prepared baking dish.

Pour both cans of apple pie filling over the batter a little at a time, being careful to spread it evenly and not all in one place. (I take a spoon and dip out a slice at a time, placing a single layer over all.)

Spread the oat mixture evenly over the pie filling. Sprinkle the cinnamon lightly over all.

Bake for 45 to 50 minutes or until golden brown. Remove and let stand at room temperature for 15 to 20 minutes before trying to cut. Serve if desired with fat-free topping or ice cream or frozen yogurt.

TROPICAL BANANA CAKE

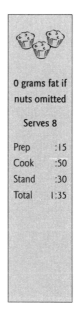

1 (12-ounce) package fat-free banana-flavored snack cake mix
2 cups water
½ cup egg substitute

TOPPING:

½ teaspoon lemon juice
2 ripe bananas, mashed
2 cups nonfat frozen whipped topping, thawed
12 maraschino cherries, chopped
½ (14-ounce) can fat-free sweetened condensed milk (*not* evaporated milk)
¼ cup chopped nuts (optional)

0 grams fat if
nuts omitted

Serves 8

Prep	:15
Cook	:50
Stand	:30
Total	1:35

Preheat the oven to 375 degrees. Lightly coat an 11 x 8½-inch baking pan with vegetable oil cooking spray.

In a mixing bowl, combine the cake mix with the water and egg substitute. Mix until thoroughly combined. Pour and scrape the batter into the prepared pan and bake for 40 to 50 minutes or until a wooden pick inserted in the center comes out clean.

While the cake is baking, prepare the topping: Add the lemon juice to the mashed bananas and mix well. Fold in the whipped topping and chopped cherries. Refrigerate until needed to complete the cake.

When the cake is done, remove it to a cooling rack and cool in the pan for about 5 minutes. Punch holes all over the cake with a fork. Pour the condensed milk evenly over the surface and let it soak into the cake while it cools completely.

Retrieve the topping from the refrigerator and spread over the cooled cake. Sprinkle with nuts if desired. Refrigerate until serving time.

BANANA SPLIT CAKE

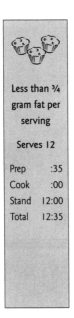

Make this the day before you plan to serve it.

Less than ¾ gram fat per serving

Serves 12

Prep	:35
Cook	:00
Stand	12:00
Total	12:35

2 cups low-fat graham crackers, crushed
½ cup pourable fat-free margarine
1 cup solid-type fat-free margarine, at room temperature
2 cups powdered sugar
½ cup egg substitute
4 bananas
2 tablespoons lemon juice
2 cups crushed pineapple, drained
1 (9-ounce) container fat-free frozen whipped topping, thawed
¼ cup chopped nuts (optional)
Maraschino cherries (optional)

Combine the graham cracker crumbs and the pourable margarine in the bowl of an electric mixer. Mix until crumbly. Press firmly into the bottom of a 13 x 9 x 2-inch baking dish. Set aside.

In the same bowl, combine the solid margarine with the powdered sugar and the egg substitute. Beat for 10 minutes at medium speed. Spread the mixture over the graham cracker crumbs.

Peel and slice the bananas thin. (I cut mine lengthwise like a banana split.) Place in a dish and sprinkle with lemon juice, turning to make sure all the slices are coated to prevent them from turning dark.

Layer the bananas over the egg mixture. Spread the pineapple over the bananas and spread the whipped topping over the pineapple. If using the chopped nuts and cherries, sprinkle over lightly to garnish. Remember the nuts will add grams of fat, so be light handed with them. The cherries are fine, use as many as you like to make it look pretty.

Refrigerate overnight. Cut into squares and serve.

CHERRY WINE CAKE

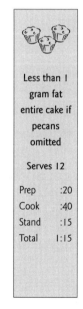

Less than 1 gram fat entire cake if pecans omitted

Serves 12

Prep	:20
Cook	:40
Stand	:15
Total	1:15

¼ cup pecans, chopped fine
1 (18¼-ounce) package reduced-fat white cake mix
1 (3-ounce) package cherry gelatin dessert mix
½ cup applesauce
1 cup egg substitute
2 cups cherry wine, divided
1 cup powdered sugar
½ cup solid-type fat-free margarine

GARNISH:

1 cup cherry pie filling (optional)
1 medium-size container frozen fat-free whipped topping, thawed (optional)

Preheat the oven to 325 degrees. Lightly coat a 13 x 9 x 2-inch glass baking dish with vegetable oil cooking spray. Sprinkle the chopped pecans evenly over the bottom of the dish.

In a medium-size mixing bowl, combine the cake mix, gelatin dessert mix, applesauce, egg substitute, and 1½ cups of the wine. Beat at high speed for 2 minutes. Pour the batter into the prepared baking dish and spread evenly.

Bake for 40 minutes or until a wooden pick inserted into the center of the cake comes out clean. Remove the cake to a wire rack and punch holes all over the surface with a fork. Let cool in the baking dish for 15 to 20 minutes or until still fairly warm to the touch.

Meanwhile, heat the remaining ½ cup of wine in a small saucepan. Add the powdered sugar and margarine and bring to a boil, stirring with a wire whisk. At boiling point, remove from the heat and pour over the warm cake.

To make the optional garnish: In a small mixing bowl, combine the cherry pie filling and whipped topping. Spread over the cake or dollop some on each serving piece. The cake is wonderful without any topping but it makes a prettier presentation if garnished with topping and maybe a couple of long-stemmed cherries in the center.

BLACK AND WHITE PUDDING POKE CAKE

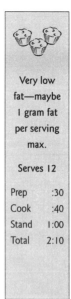

1 package low-fat chocolate cake mix, such as Sweet Rewards
1⅓ cups water
2 tablespoons applesauce
¾ cup egg substitute
4 cups fat-free milk
2 (4-ounce) packages vanilla-flavored instant pudding mix
½ teaspoon cocoa powder for garnish if desired

Very low
fat—maybe
1 gram fat
per serving
max.

Serves 12

Prep	:30
Cook	:40
Stand	1:00
Total	2:10

Preheat the oven to 350 degrees. Lightly spray a 13 x 9 x 2-inch baking dish with vegetable oil cooking spray.

In a mixing bowl, combine the cake mix with the water, applesauce, and egg substitute. Beat with an electric mixer until blended. Pour into the prepared baking dish. Bake for 40 to 45 minutes or until a wooden pick inserted in the center of the cake comes out clean.

Immediately after removing the cake from the oven, poke holes in the top with a wooden spoon handle or a drinking straw about every inch or two. Turn the handle of the spoon or the straw to make holes large enough for your pudding to go down into them.

Pour the milk into a large mixing bowl and add the pudding mixes. Beat with a wire whisk for about 2 minutes. Very quickly, before the pudding starts to thicken, pour it over the cake evenly, letting the pudding run down into the holes, just filling them. Let the remaining pudding stand just a couple minutes or until it starts to thicken. Spread the remaining pudding over the cake, making nice swirls to decorate it. Sprinkle a little cocoa over to garnish.

HOT FUDGE SUNDAE PUDDING CAKE

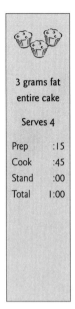

**3 grams fat
entire cake**

Serves 4

Prep	:15
Cook	:45
Stand	:00
Total	1:00

This is another recipe from my first book I have added just to make sure if you only have the dessert book you will have this cake. It is to die for.

1 cup all-purpose flour

2 teaspoons baking powder

¼ teaspoon salt (optional)

¾ cup granulated sugar

¼ cup plus 1½ tablespoons unsweetened cocoa powder, divided

½ cup fat-free milk

2 tablespoons pourable low-fat margarine

1 teaspoon vanilla extract

¼ cup finely chopped nuts (optional)

¾ cup packed brown sugar

1¾ cups boiling water

Preheat the oven to 350 degrees. Prepare a 9-inch square baking pan by lightly spraying with vegetable oil cooking spray. (If a larger cake is wanted for entertaining, double the recipe and use a 9 x 13 x 2-inch baking dish.)

In a large bowl, combine the flour, baking powder, salt, sugar, and 1½ tablespoons of cocoa powder; mix well. Add the milk, margarine, and vanilla; stir until well blended. Stir in the nuts if using. The mixture will be slightly thick. Spread in the prepared pan.

Mix the brown sugar and the remaining ¼ cup of cocoa; sprinkle over the cake batter. *Do not stir.*

Pour the hot water over the cocoa. *Do not stir.*

Bake for 40 to 45 minutes. To serve, cut into squares while still hot and invert each piece onto an individual dish. Top with fat-free yogurt or ice cream. Spoon chocolate sauce from the bottom of the pan over the ice cream or yogurt.

Yum!! I just cannot tell you how good this is and how easy.

BANANA NUT CAKE

3 ripe bananas
¼ cup solid-type fat-free margarine
1 tablespoon pourable low-fat margarine
1½ cups granulated sugar
½ cup egg substitute
1 (6-ounce) jar banana baby food
1 teaspoon baking soda
4 tablespoons low-fat buttermilk
1½ cups all-purpose flour
¼ cup finely chopped nuts (optional)
1 teaspoon vanilla extract

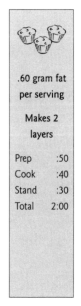

.60 gram fat
per serving

Makes 2
layers

Prep	:50
Cook	:40
Stand	:30
Total	2:00

Preheat the oven to 350 degrees. Spray two 9-inch cake pans lightly with vegetable oil cooking spray; dust lightly with flour, shaking out any excess, and set pans aside.

In a shallow dish, such as a pie plate, mash bananas with a fork.

Cream the margarines and sugar together in a large mixing bowl. In a small bowl, beat the egg substitute with an electric mixer until foamy; add to the sugar mixture. Combine the banana baby food and mashed bananas. Add half the banana mixture to the sugar and egg mixture.

Add the soda to the buttermilk, stir, and add to the banana mixture, mixing to blend evenly. Add the rest of the bananas, the flour, nuts if using, and vanilla. Continue to mix until well blended.

Pour half the batter in each of the prepared cake pans. Bake for 30 to 40 minutes or until the cake springs back when touched or a toothpick inserted near the center comes out clean. Let cool in the pans on a wire rack for 10 minutes. Loosen edges of cakes, invert on the rack, and remove the pans. Turn cakes right side up and let cool completely. Frost with your favorite frosting.

LEMONLICIOUS CAKE

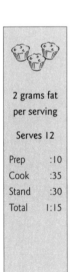

2 grams fat
per serving

Serves 12

Prep :10
Cook :35
Stand :30
Total 1:15

1 (18¼-ounce) package reduced-fat yellow cake mix
2 cups boiling water
1 (6-ounce) package sugar-free lemon-flavored gelatin desert
Fluffy lemon pudding frosting (page 106)

Prepare the cake following the no-cholesterol package directions, using egg substitute and applesauce instead of eggs and vegetable oil.

Bake as directed in 2 round pans or in a 13 x 9 x 2-inch pan lightly sprayed with vegetable oil cooking spray. When the cake is done to the touch, remove from the oven. Let cool in the pans for 10 minutes. Turn out of pans onto wire racks and cool completely. Put cakes back into pans. (If using 1 large pan you can leave in the pan but cool completely.)

Punch holes in the cake with a fork.

In a medium bowl, stir the boiling water into the gelatin mix until dissolved. Pour over the cake; if you have a two-layer cake, divide the gelatin mixture equally between the cakes. Refrigerate at least 3 hours. Meanwhile make the frosting.

When ready to frost, if making a layer cake, dip the bottom of the pan in hot water for 10 seconds. Unmold onto a cake plate. Spread with about 1 cup of frosting for the first layer, placing the second layer on top of the first; frost sides first, then the top.

Garnish if desired with a slice of lemon standing with mint leaves around the sides and around the lemon slice.

AUTUMN PUMPKIN CAKE

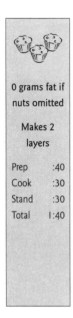

0 grams fat if
nuts omitted

Makes 2
layers

Prep   :40
Cook   :30
Stand   :30
Total   1:40

½ cup applesauce
1 cup granulated sugar
1 cup packed brown sugar
½ cup egg substitute
1 cup canned solid-pack pumpkin
3 cups cake flour
4 teaspoons baking powder
¼ teaspoon baking soda
½ cup fat-free milk
¼ cup chopped nuts (optional)
1 teaspoon maple extract

Preheat the oven to 350 degrees. Lightly spray with cooking spray and lightly flour two 9-inch round cake pans; knock out excess flour.

In a large bowl, beat together the applesauce, granulated sugar, and brown sugar. Add the egg substitute and pumpkin and blend thoroughly.

Combine the flour, baking powder, and baking soda and whisk until well mixed. Add the flour mixture alternately with the milk to the pumpkin mixture, beginning and ending with flour. Beat well after each addition. Fold in the nuts if using and the maple extract. Stir well.

Pour into the prepared cake pans and bake for 30 minutes or until the cake springs back when touched lightly. Let cool in the pans for 10 minutes, then turn out of pans onto a wire rack and let cool completely. Frost with Harvest Moon Frosting, page 103.

MYRNA'S MAGIC MANDARIN CAKE

This recipe came from one of my ladies who has lost 100 pounds and 60 inches by using my cookbooks. Congratulations, Myrna.

½ cup egg substitute
⅓ cup unsweetened applesauce
1 (18¼-ounce) package reduced-fat yellow cake mix
1 (11-ounce) can mandarin oranges, undrained

FROSTING:

1 (3-ounce) package fat-free vanilla instant pudding mix
1 (12-ounce) container fat-free frozen whipped topping, thawed
1 (8-ounce) can crushed pineapple, undrained
Small jar orange marmalade for garnish (optional)

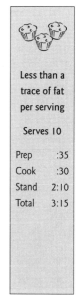

Less than a
trace of fat
per serving

Serves 10

Prep	:35
Cook	:30
Stand	2:10
Total	3:15

Preheat the oven to 325 degrees. Lightly spray two 9-inch round cake pans with vegetable oil cooking spray. Dust the pans with flour, shaking out any excess.

Combine the egg substitute, applesauce, cake mix, and mandarin oranges in a medium mixing bowl. With an electric mixer, beat slowly for about 30 seconds, then turn mixer to medium high and continue to beat for 2 additional minutes.

Pour the batter into the prepared pans. Bake for 30 minutes or until a toothpick inserted in the center of the cakes comes out clean. Let cool for 10 minutes in the pans, then turn out of pans and cool completely on a wire rack.

To make the frosting, beat together the pudding mix, whipped topping, and pineapple until thickened.

(recipe continues)

Center one of the cakes right side up on a serving dish. Cover the top with frosting. Place the second layer right side up over the first. Frost the sides first, then the top. Or if desired, cover the top only with orange marmalade and use the remaining frosting to dollop or spread in a ring on the outside of the top of the cake.

Chill for at least 2 hours before serving.

MOCHA BUTTERMILK CAKE

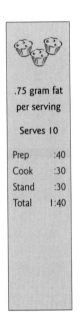

.75 gram fat
per serving

Serves 10

Prep	:40
Cook	:30
Stand	:30
Total	1:40

1 tablespoon reduced-fat margarine
1½ cups granulated sugar
½ cup applesauce
3 tablespoons strong hot coffee
¼ cup unsweetened cocoa powder
¼ cup egg substitute
1 teaspoon baking soda
1 cup low-fat buttermilk
1½ teaspoons vanilla extract
2 cups all-purpose flour
¼ teaspoon salt (optional)

Preheat the oven to 350 degrees. Lightly spray two 9-inch round baking pans with vegetable oil cooking spray.

Cream together the margarine, sugar, and applesauce in a large bowl with an electric mixer. Add the coffee and beat until mixed. Add the cocoa and beat, then add the egg substitute. Mix until well blended.

Combine the baking soda, buttermilk, and vanilla in a separate small bowl or cup. In another bowl, whisk the flour and salt together. Add the flour to the cocoa mixture alternately with the buttermilk mixture, beginning and ending with flour and beating well after each addition.

Pour the batter into the prepared cake pans. Bake for 25 to 30 minutes or until a toothpick inserted in the center of the cakes comes out clean. Let cool in the pans for 5 to 10 minutes, then turn out of the pans to cool on a wire rack.

Frost with your favorite low-fat frosting.

FAUX COCONUT CHOCOLATE CAKE

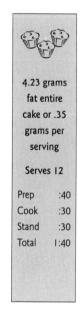

4.23 grams
fat entire
cake or .35
grams per
serving

Serves 12

Prep	:40
Cook	:30
Stand	:30
Total	1:40

⅔ cup solid-type fat-free margarine

1½ cups sugar

1 teaspoon vanilla extract

2½ cups all-purpose flour

½ cup unsweetened cocoa powder

1 teaspoon baking powder

1 teaspoon baking soda

¼ teaspoon salt (optional)

¾ cup egg substitute

1 cup water

⅔ cup sauerkraut, rinsed and drained

MOCHA TOPPING:

1½ to 2 cups fat-free frozen whipped topping, thawed

3 tablespoons sugar

1 tablespoon instant coffee granules

2 teaspoons unsweetened cocoa powder

Preheat the oven to 350 degrees. Coat two 8-inch round cake pans with vegetable oil cooking spray and dust with flour, tapping out excess.

In a large mixing bowl, beat the margarine and sugar together until fluffy. Beat in the vanilla. Set aside.

In another bowl, combine the flour, cocoa, baking powder, baking soda, and salt. Whisk until thoroughly mixed.

Combine the egg substitute and water in a measuring cup.

Alternately add the flour mixture and the water to the margarine mixture, beginning and ending with flour. Beat well after each addition. Stir in the sauerkraut.

Divide the batter as equally as possible between the two pans. Bake for 25 to 30 minutes or until a wooden pick inserted in the center of the cakes comes out clean. Let cool in the pans for 5 to 10 minutes, then turn out of the pans and allow to cool completely.

Make the topping: Combine the whipped topping, sugar, coffee granules, and cocoa; beat together until mixed. Taste and add ¼ teaspoon of vanilla if desired.

Place one cake layer on a serving plate and cover the top with frosting. Place the second layer over the frosting. Frost the sides of the cake and then the top. Garnish if desired with a couple of long-stemmed cherries or a small chocolate curl.

CHOCOLATE LOG CAKE

1 cup egg substitute
½ teaspoon vanilla extract
¾ cup granulated sugar
4 large egg whites, at room temperature
¾ cup all-purpose flour
1 teaspoon baking powder
¼ teaspoon salt
Powdered sugar for dusting
Low-Fat Chocolate Frosting (page 107)
½ cup ground nuts (optional)

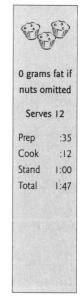

0 grams fat if
nuts omitted

Serves 12

Prep	:35
Cook	:12
Stand	1:00
Total	1:47

Preheat the oven to 375 degrees. Line the bottom of a 15½ x 10½ x 1-inch jelly roll pan with waxed paper.

In a large bowl, with an electric mixer on low speed, beat the egg substitute until slightly thickened. Increase speed to moderate. Gradually beat in the vanilla and ¼ cup of the sugar, a tablespoon at a time.

In a different bowl, squeaky clean and preferably glass, and with clean beaters, beat the egg whites until foamy. Gradually add the remaining ½ cup of granulated sugar, beating on moderate speed until soft, glossy peaks are formed.

Sift or whisk the flour, baking powder, and salt together. Fold the egg whites into the egg substitute. Sift the flour mixture over the whites and fold in gently, one or two tablespoons at a time.

Pour the mixture into the prepared pan and tilt or spread to even the surface. Bake for 12 minutes.

(recipe continues)

Remove from the oven and invert onto a towel sprinkled with powdered sugar. Remove the waxed paper and quickly roll up with fresh waxed paper put on top or the inside as you roll it. This will keep the cake from sticking to itself.

Cool completely, about 1 hour. Unroll the cake, removing the paper, and spread with low-fat chocolate frosting. Roll up, starting with a short end, and frost with remaining frosting. Sprinkle with nuts while the frosting is still hot, if desired.

PINEAPPLE UPSIDE-DOWN JELLY ROLL

Slight trace of fat from the oats and cooking spray

Serves 8

Prep   :20
Cook   :30
Stand   :05
Total   :55

¼ cup uncooked rolled oats
¼ cup packed brown sugar
1 cup applesauce
1 cup crushed pineapple, drained
4 egg whites
1 teaspoon vanilla extract
⅔ cup granulated sugar
⅔ cup all-purpose flour
¾ teaspoon baking powder
Pinch of salt
Powdered sugar for dusting

Preheat the oven to 375 degrees. Lightly coat a 15½ x 10½ x 1-inch jelly roll pan with vegetable oil cooking spray. Line the bottom and sides with wide aluminum foil, making little side boards on the side of the pan, and spray the foil lightly.

In a large mixing bowl, combine the oats, brown sugar, applesauce, and pineapple. Stir until mixed thoroughly. Pour into the foil-lined pan and spread out evenly over the entire pan.

In a clear glass mixing bowl with clean beaters, beat the egg whites on low speed until foamy. Add the vanilla. Gradually add the granulated sugar, a tablespoon at a time, heating on moderate speed until the whites stand in soft peaks.

In a separate bowl, combine the flour, baking powder, and salt; stir with a whisk to blend. Start folding the flour into the egg whites with a spatula, one or two tablespoons at a time, just until smooth.

Carefully and slowly pour the batter over the pineapple layer, spreading to cover it all. Bake for 25 to 30 minutes or until a toothpick inserted in the center comes out clean. Remove from the oven and let stand for 5 minutes.

Meanwhile, spread a clean kitchen towel out on a work surface and sprinkle it with powdered sugar. Flip the cake over onto the cloth, carefully raise the pan up, and remove the foil. If any of the topping is stuck to the foil, at this time remove it and spread it back onto the cake in the bare spots.

Carefully pick up the cloth at one end. Start rolling from narrow end to narrow end; keep lifting up on the cloth end, using it to do the rolling. (Not too fast or you will break your jelly roll, and I can't think of anything worse than a cracked jelly roll.) When rolled, place the cake on a serving platter, seam side down. Serve as is, or you may wish to make a glaze to drizzle over.

Note: Do you know why they always say to blend the flour and all the dry ingredients together before adding to a wet mixture? So you won't get a mouthful of salt or soda or whatever you may be blending with the flour before adding to the batter.

EASY CHOCOLATE ROLL-UP

.26 gram fat
per serving

Serves 10

Prep	:30
Cook	:20
Stand	:04
Total	:54

¼ cup pourable fat-free margarine
1 cup fat-free granola without fruit
1 (14-ounce) can fat-free sweetened condensed milk
   (*not* evaporated milk)

CAKE:

¾ cup egg substitute
1 cup granulated sugar
⅓ cup unsweetened cocoa powder
⅔ cup all-purpose flour
¼ teaspoon salt (optional)
¼ teaspoon baking soda
⅓ cup water
1 teaspoon vanilla extract
Powdered sugar for dusting

Preheat the oven to 375 degrees. Spray a 15½ x 10½ x 1-inch jelly roll pan with vegetable oil cooking spray; line the bottom and sides of the pan with aluminum foil. Brush the margarine evenly over the foil and sprinkle the granola evenly over the margarine. Drizzle with the condensed milk. Set aside.

Make the cake: In a mixing bowl, beat the egg substitute at high speed for 2 minutes or until fluffy. Gradually add the sugar and continue beating for 2 additional minutes.

In a small bowl, combine the cocoa, flour, salt, and baking soda. Whisk to blend thoroughly. In a measuring cup, mix the water and vanilla.

Add the flour mixture to the egg mixture alternately with the liquid, beginning and ending with the flour and beating well after each addition. Pour the batter into the prepared pan and bake for 20 to 25 minutes or until the cake springs back when lightly touched in the center.

Cool for 3 or 4 minutes, sprinkle the cake with powdered sugar to keep towel from sticking, cover with a clean towel and invert on a rack. Remove pan and foil. Starting with a 10 inch side, roll up jelly roll fashion, using the towel to roll the cake. (Do not roll the towel in the cake.) Leave wrapped until cooled.

Transfer to a serving dish. Drizzle with powdered sugar drizzle or chocolate drizzle (page 108).

BANANA PUDDING APPLESAUCE CAKE

0 grams fat if
cookies
omitted

Serves 10

Prep	:25
Cook	:00
Stand	1:00
Total	1:25

1 purchased angel food cake (tube form) without frosting
2 medium-size bananas
2 teaspoons lemon juice
1 (0.9-ounce) package fat-free sugar-free instant banana
   pudding mix
2 cups fat-free milk
6 to 8 low-fat vanilla wafers (optional)
1 cup applesauce

Using a thin long-bladed sharp knife, slice the cake into 4 or 5 circular layers (don't bother to unstack). Turn the entire stack upside down onto a plate until ready to assemble.

Slice the bananas into thin rounds, sprinkle lemon juice over, and toss to coat all.

In a medium-size mixing bowl, combine the pudding mix and milk. Stir with a wire whisk until thickened.

Crush the vanilla wafers if you choose to use them. (I use a food processor.) Set aside.

Start assembly:

Layer 1. Place the bottom cake layer on a serving dish or cake plate. Spread a layer of applesauce, about ⅓ cup, over the cake.

Layer 2. Place a second layer of cake over the applesauce. Spread a thin layer of the pudding mix over the cake, a layer of bananas, and a couple of additional table-spoons of applesauce over the bananas.

3. Repeat layer one.

4. Repeat layer two.

5. Ending layer. Spread with remaining applesauce. Combine remaining pudding mix and bananas. Spread over the top. Sprinkle with cookie crumbs if using.

Refrigerate at least an hour before serving.

Variations:

Substitute a different fruit for banana, such as drained pineapple. (Tease: Of course you do know that if you use a different fruit it is no longer banana pudding—it will be fruit pudding applesauce cake.)

CLOUD-FILLED ANGEL FOOD CAKE

0 grams fat if nuts omitted

Makes 1 cake

Prep	:30
Cook	:00
Stand	1:00
Total	1:30

You can freeze this or serve it as soon as chilled. Make ahead or when you please.

1 purchased angel food cake without frosting
1 (14-ounce) can fat-free sweetened condensed milk (*not* evaporated milk)
1 (21-ounce) can crushed pineapple, drained
1 (12-ounce) package fat-free frozen whipped topping, thawed
1 (3-ounce) package instant white chocolate pudding mix
1 cup small marshmallows
¼ cup chopped maraschino cherries
¼ cup finely chopped nuts (optional)

Slice the angel food cake with a sharp knife about ⅓ of the way down, making a thick top slice. Set the top slice to one side. Take a knife and remove the center of the cake, slicing a circle on the inside. Cut the center into small bite-size pieces. Set aside.

In a large mixing bowl, combine the condensed milk, drained crushed pineapple, whipped topping, and pudding mix, stirring all the while. Continue mixing, while you add the cake pieces, marshmallows, cherries, and nuts if using.

Fill the center of the cake with the pineapple mixture. Put the slice from the top back on, frost inside the hole with some of the remaining mixture, then frost the outside and top of the cake. Place in refrigerator or freezer at least 1 hour before serving. Allow to stand at room temperature for about 30 minutes, or at least 30 minutes if it has come from the freezer.

Frostings, Toppings, and Sauces

"BUTTERCREAM" FROSTING

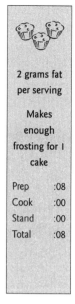

5⅓ tablespoons (⅓ cup) reduced-fat margarine, at room temperature
3½ to 4 cups powdered sugar
Pinch of salt
I teaspoon vanilla extract or flavoring of your choice
3 tablespoons fat-free milk or coffee

Combine the margarine and sugar in a small bowl. Blend. Add the salt and flavoring. Start adding milk or coffee 1 tablespoon at a time until the mixture has a spreadable consistency.

2 grams fat per serving	
Makes enough frosting for I cake	
Prep	:08
Cook	:00
Stand	:00
Total	:08

BURNT SUGAR FROSTING

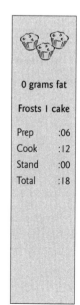

I cup granulated sugar
¾ cup boiling water
¼ cup egg whites
¼ teaspoon cream of tartar
Dash of salt

Put the sugar in a heavy pan, such as a dry cast iron skillet. Stir constantly with a wooden spoon over moderate heat until the sugar melts and turns caramel colored.

Remove the pan from the heat. Carefully add boiling water—stand back to avoid being scalded—and return to the heat. Add the egg whites, cream of tartar, and salt. Continue to cook, stirring constantly until mixed. Cook and stir until caramelized.

0 grams fat	
Frosts I cake	
Prep	:06
Cook	:12
Stand	:00
Total	:18

SEVEN-MINUTE FROSTING

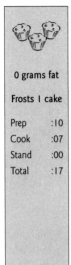

0 grams fat

Frosts 1 cake

Prep	:10
Cook	:07
Stand	:00
Total	:17

2 egg whites
Dash of salt
1 tablespoon light corn syrup
1½ cups granulated sugar
½ cup cold water
1 teaspoon vanilla extract

In the top of a double boiler, combine the egg whites, salt, corn syrup, sugar, and water. With an electric mixer, start beating to blend. Beat 1 minute, then place over boiling water. Continue to beat at high speed for 4 to 6 minutes or until stiff peaks form. Remove from heat and beat in vanilla. Makes enough to frost a 2-layer 9-inch cake.

Variations:

Peppermint frosting:
Omit vanilla and substitute 8 or 9 drops peppermint extract and a couple drops red or green food coloring.

Maple Frosting:
Substitute maple flavoring for vanilla.

Lemon frosting:
Substitute lemon extract for vanilla and add yellow food coloring.

HARVEST MOON FROSTING

3 large egg whites
1½ cups firmly packed brown sugar
Pinch of salt
6 tablespoons cold water
1 teaspoon vanilla extract

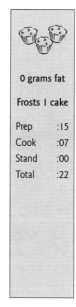

0 grams fat

Frosts 1 cake

Prep	:15
Cook	:07
Stand	:00
Total	:22

In the top half of a double boiler, combine the egg whites, brown sugar, salt, and water. Start beating on low with an electric mixer. Place over boiling water and cook seven minutes, beating constantly, until the frosting stands in stiff peaks. Remove from heat. Add vanilla. Beat until thick enough to spread on cake.

Place one layer of cake on a serving dish, frost the top; place the second layer over the first. Frost the sides, then the top.

Garnish with a tiny candy pumpkin or candy corn if desired.

CREAM CHEESE FROSTING I

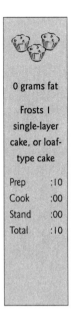

0 grams fat

Frosts I
single-layer
cake, or loaf-
type cake

Prep   :10
Cook   :00
Stand   :00
Total   :10

I (6-ounce) package fat-free cream cheese, at room temperature
½ cup solid-type fat-free margarine, at room temperature
I teaspoon vanilla extract
3½ to 4 cups powdered sugar

   With a wire whisk, very carefully, mix the cream cheese, margarine, and vanilla. Be careful—the cheese will get too thin if mixed too hard. Gradually add the powdered sugar, whisking until smooth and of spreading consistency.

   Refrigerate after frosting your cake and refrigerate any cake left over.

CREAM CHEESE FROSTING II

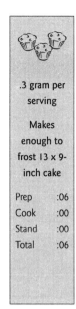

I (8-ounce) package fat-free cream cheese
I ½ cups fat-free ricotta cheese
⅓ cup granulated sugar
I tablespoon lemon juice
I teaspoon vanilla extract
2 tablespoons instant vanilla pudding mix

.3 gram per
serving

Makes
enough to
frost 13 x 9-
inch cake

Prep	:06
Cook	:00
Stand	:00
Total	:06

Place the cheeses in a blender and process until smooth.

Add the sugar, lemon juice, and vanilla. Blend just a few seconds.

Add the pudding mix. Pulse or blend just enough to blend. Remove from blender; frost cake.

Refrigerate after frosting your cake and refrigerate any cake left over.

FLUFFY LEMON PUDDING FROSTING

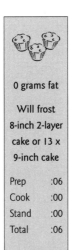

0 grams fat

Will frost
8-inch 2-layer
cake or 13 x
9-inch cake

Prep	:06
Cook	:00
Stand	:00
Total	:06

I cup fat-free milk
I (4-ounce) package instant lemon pudding mix
¼ cup powdered sugar
I (8-ounce) tub frozen fat-free whipped topping, thawed

Pour the milk into a bowl. Stir in the pudding and pow-dered sugar. Beat with a wire whisk to blend. Stir in the whipped topping until blended well.

LOW-FAT CHOCOLATE FROSTING

¼ cup boiling water
¼ cup low-fat chocolate chips
¼ cup unsweetened cocoa powder
3 tablespoons fat-free margarine
¾ cup egg substitute
I teaspoon vanilla extract
2 to 2½ cups powdered sugar
3 tablespoons cornstarch

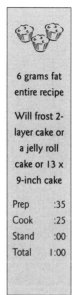

6 grams fat
entire recipe

Will frost 2-
layer cake or
a jelly roll
cake or 13 x
9-inch cake

Prep	:35
Cook	:25
Stand	:00
Total	1:00

Place water, chocolate chips, cocoa, and margarine in a saucepan. Place over low heat and cook until chocolate is melted. Add vanilla and egg substitute. Stir well while cooking.

In a large bowl, mix sugar and cornstarch, blending well. Add all at once to hot chocolate mixture. Stir over heat just until thick. You may need to add a little extra powdered sugar for desired consistency. Spread on cake while hot.

CHOCOLATE DRIZZLE OR GLAZE

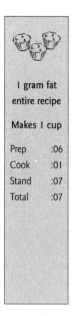

I gram fat
entire recipe

Makes I cup

Prep   :06
Cook   :01
Stand   :07
Total   :07

2 cups powdered sugar
2 tablespoons unsweetened cocoa powder
3 tablespoons fat-free milk

Combine all the ingredients in a small saucepan. Heat until runny, stirring with a wire whisk constantly, about 1 minute.

Pour over a favorite dessert.

For a powdered sugar drizzle, omit the cocoa and add 2 tablespoons more powdered sugar.

HOT FRUIT SAUCE

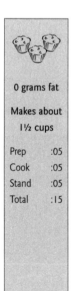

0 grams fat

Makes about
I ½ cups

Prep   :05
Cook   :05
Stand   :05
Total   :15

I cup canned fruit pie filling, chopped
¼ teaspoon vanilla extract
¼ cup coconut amaretto
2 tablespoons packed brown sugar

In a small saucepan, combine the fruit, vanilla, amaretto, and brown sugar. Blend well with a wire whisk. Place over medium high heat. Bring to a boil, lower the heat, and continue on a low boil, stirring all the while until the sauce thickens. Remove from the heat and let cool just about 5 minutes. Spoon over cake or pudding. If cake, let it drizzle down the sides. Serve with fat-free ice cream or frozen yogurt if desired.

PINEAPPLE GLAZE

1 (8-ounce) can crushed pineapple
1 teaspoon granulated sugar
1 teaspoon cornstarch

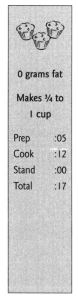

0 grams fat

Makes ¾ to 1 cup

Prep	:05
Cook	:12
Stand	:00
Total	:17

Combine the pineapple and its juice in a small saucepan with the cornstarch and sugar. Place over moderate heat and stir constantly with a wire whisk until the consistency of waffle syrup.

Drizzle over any dessert, or let cool and pour over fat-free frozen yogurt or ice cream.

CUSTARD SAUCE

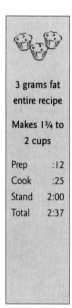

**3 grams fat
entire recipe**

**Makes 1¾ to
2 cups**

Prep	:12
Cook	:25
Stand	2:00
Total	2:37

¾ cup egg substitute
1 egg yolk
¼ cup granulated sugar
Pinch of salt (optional)
2 cups undiluted fat-free evaporated milk, scalded
1 teaspoon vanilla extract

In the top part of a double boiler, combine the egg substitute, egg yolk, sugar, and salt. Place over boiling water. With a wire whisk, start stirring; gradually stir in the scalded milk. Continue to cook over the hot water over medium heat, stirring constantly, until the mixture starts to thicken or coat the whisk. Add the vanilla; stir to blend well. Remove from the heat when thickened to your preference. Serve over plain cake or bread pudding.

Hint: If your sauce does not thicken as much as you want, you can dissolve 1 teaspoon of cornstarch in 2 tablespoons of cold water, then gradually stir into the sauce as you continue to cook. Be careful—don't dump it all at once into the sauce or you will need to slice your sauce for serving.

LEMON SAUCE

This can be made ahead and stored in the refrigerator for up to four days. Before serving, warm carefully so as not to scorch.

1 cup granulated sugar
2 tablespoons cornstarch
2 cups cold water
1 tablespoon light margarine
3 tablespoons fresh lemon zest (grated lemon peel)
¼ cup fresh lemon juice

4.5 grams fat
entire recipe

Serves 6

Prep	:05
Cook	:05
Stand	:00
Total	:10

Mix the sugar and cornstarch; blend well with a wire whisk in a small saucepan. Add the cold water, stir to dissolve, and place over medium heat. Continue to stir until boiling; lower the heat to medium low, and continue to boil, stirring all the while, until thickened and translucent.

Remove from the heat and stir in the margarine, lemon zest, and lemon juice. Stir to blend well.

Serve warm over a favorite dessert.

CARAMEL SAUCE

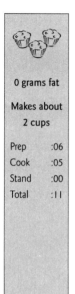

0 grams fat

Makes about
2 cups

Prep	:06
Cook	:05
Stand	:00
Total	:11

1 (8-ounce) package fat-free cream cheese, softened
½ cup packed brown sugar
½ teaspoon vanilla extract
½ teaspoon amaretto (optional)

In a medium nonstick saucepan, combine the cheese and brown sugar. Stir with a whisk to blend; place over medium heat until the mixture starts to warm. Add the vanilla and amaretto; stir to blend.

Serve over fat-free frozen yogurt, ice cream, or fresh fruit, or use for dipping fruit.

CHOCO-RUM SAUCE

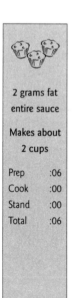

2 grams fat
entire sauce

Makes about
2 cups

Prep	:06
Cook	:00
Stand	:00
Total	:06

4 cups powdered sugar
Pinch of salt
¼ cup unsweetened cocoa powder
⅓ cup (5⅓ tablespoons) reduced-fat margarine, softened
1 teaspoon rum flavoring
¼ cup hot water

Mix the sugar, salt, and cocoa in a small bowl. Stir in the margarine and rum flavoring, and add 1 tablespoon of water at a time until the sauce reaches the desired consistency.

RUM SAUCE FOR CAKES OR DESSERTS

1 ½ cups granulated sugar
⅔ cup light corn syrup
½ cup cold water
⅓ cup rum

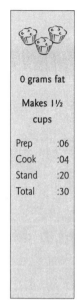

0 grams fat

Makes 1 ½ cups

Prep	:06
Cook	:04
Stand	:20
Total	:30

In a small saucepan, combine the sugar, corn syrup, and water. Stir with a whisk until well blended. Place over medium heat, stirring; bring to a low simmer, and let simmer for about 4 minutes.

Remove from the heat, add the rum, stir, and let stand about 20 minutes

APPLE CIDER SAUCE

½ cup packed brown sugar
¼ cup pourable fat-free margarine
¼ cup apple cider
2 tablespoons undiluted fat-free evaporated milk

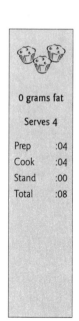

0 grams fat

Serves 4

Prep	:04
Cook	:04
Stand	:00
Total	:08

In a heavy nonstick saucepan, bring all ingredients to a full rolling boil over moderate heat, stirring constantly. Reduce the heat and boil for 3 to 4 minutes, stirring frequently. Watch and stir carefully—the mixture burns easily.

SWEET CREAM CHEESE SPREAD

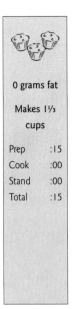

0 grams fat

Makes 1⅓ cups

Prep	:15
Cook	:00
Stand	:00
Total	:15

1 (8-ounce) container fat-free cream cheese, softened
½ cup chopped dried apricots
½ cup chopped dried cranberries (or fresh)
1 teaspoon orange zest (grated orange peel)

Put the cream cheese in a bowl and add the apricots, cranberries, and orange zest. Stir gently with a spatula or wooden spoon until blended. Be careful not to overwork—fat-free cream cheese breaks down easily. Serve as a sweet spread for breads and party crackers.

Variation:

Combine the cream cheese with ½ cup chopped dried dates, ¼ cup chopped nuts, and ¼ cup chopped maraschino cherries.

FRUIT DIP

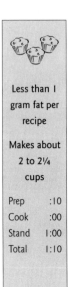

Less than 1 gram fat per recipe

Makes about 2 to 2¼ cups

Prep	:10
Cook	:00
Stand	1:00
Total	1:10

1 (8-ounce) package fat-free cream cheese, at room temperature
⅔ cup packed brown sugar
¾ cup fat-free sour cream
2 teaspoons vanilla extract
1 teaspoon lemon juice
1 cup fat-free milk
1 (3-ounce) package instant vanilla pudding mix
Assorted fresh fruit

Combine the cream cheese and brown sugar in a bowl and mix carefully with a wire whisk, stirring gently until smooth. Add the sour cream, vanilla, lemon juice, and milk. Gradually start adding the pudding mix. Continue to stir until well blended. Chill at least 1 hour before serving.

Make an arrangement of seasonal fresh fruit in a ring around your bowl of dip.

HOT CHOCOLATE DIP

This may also be used as a topping for desserts such as parfaits, ice cream pies, or sliced fresh fruit.

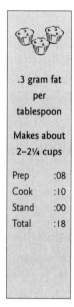

.3 gram fat per tablespoon

Makes about 2–2¼ cups

Prep	:08
Cook	:10
Stand	:00
Total	:18

¾ cup unsweetened cocoa powder
1½ cups packed brown sugar
2 tablespoons cornstarch
1⅓ cups fat-free milk
2 teaspoons vanilla extract
1 tablespoon coconut amaretto

In a medium-size nonstick saucepan, combine the cocoa, brown sugar, and cornstarch. Add the skim milk and stir with a wire whisk to blend. Place over medium heat and cook, stirring constantly, until the mixture begins to thicken. Be careful not to cook until too thick—just enough to make a nice consistency for dipping.

Remove from the heat; stir in the vanilla and amaretto.

Serve warm with fresh fruit for dipping such as strawberries, chunks of fresh pineapple, apple, banana, or cubes of poundcake or angel food cake.

Cheesecakes

PUMPKIN CHEESECAKE

Spiced Crumb Crust (page 212)
1 (8-ounce) package light cream cheese, softened
1 (8-ounce) package fat-free cream cheese, softened
⅔ cup granulated sugar
1 teaspoon vanilla extract
¾ cup egg substitute
1 (15-ounce) can solid-pack pumpkin
¾ teaspoon ground cinnamon
¼ teaspoon ground nutmeg

4 grams fat
per serving

Serves 12

Prep	:20
Cook	1:05
Stand	1:00
Total	2:25

Preheat the oven to 350 degrees. Combine crumb crust ingredients according to the recipe; press onto the bottom and 1½ inches up the sides of a 9-inch springform pan. Bake for 10 minutes.

Combine the light and the fat-free cream cheeses in a bowl; blend carefully. Add ⅓ cup of the sugar and the vanilla. Blend. With a wire whisk or an electric mixer on low speed, add the egg substitute, mixing well. Add the remaining sugar, the pumpkin, and the spices. Stir to blend. Pour into the prepared crust and bake at 350 degrees for 55 to 60 minutes or until set in the middle.

When the cheesecake is removed from the oven, take a sharp knife and loosen the edges but cool in the pan completely before removing. Chill and serve chilled.

Variations:

You may wish to choose different kinds of crumbs for the crust, such as low-fat chocolate wafers, gingersnaps, or vanilla wafers, or the regular graham cracker crust, low-fat of course. See page 213 for a homemade graham cracker crust. Watch out for those grams looking for your back-

side. Can't turn your back on them for one minute. They're kind of like chiggers: can't see them, can't hear them, can't find them, but they are there looking to get on you.

MINI PUMPKIN CHEESECAKES

This dessert may be made into individual muffins or may be made into a bar-type dessert.

1 cup low-fat baking mix, such as Bisquick
¾ cup rolled oats
1 cup packed brown sugar
½ teaspoon ground cinnamon
2 tablespoons low-fat margarine, chilled

PUMPKIN FILLING:

2 (8-ounce) packages fat-free cream cheese, at room temperature
1 (15-ounce) can solid-pack pumpkin
½ cup egg substitute
1 teaspoon vanilla extract
½ cup packed brown sugar
½ teaspoon ground cinnamon
½ teaspoon ground ginger
½ teaspoon ground nutmeg

1.84 grams per muffin-size serving

Makes 36 mini cheesecakes

Prep   :35
Cook   :25
Stand   2:30
Total   3:30

Preheat the oven to 350 degrees. Lightly coat muffin tins or an 8- or 9-inch springform pan with vegetable oil cooking spray. (I actually make 1 dozen muffin-size cheesecakes and use the rest of the ingredients in my smallest springform.)

Place the baking mix, oats, brown sugar, and cinnamon in the container of a blender or food processor. Blend until crumbly, or the consistency of heavy meal. Add the margarine, which you have cut into small chunks, to the mixture in the blender; pulse until moistened.

Place about 2 tablespoons of the crumb mixture in the bottom of each muffin tin and pat down with your fingers, or pour half the crumb mixture into the springform pan if making a large cheesecake. Pat down with fingers, dipping your fingers into sugar to keep crumbs from sticking to your fingers or spoon. Reserve the remaining crumbs for topping.

To make the filling: In a blender or food processor, combine the cream cheese, pumpkin, egg substitute, vanilla, brown sugar, cinnamon, ginger, and nutmeg. Blend or process until smooth.

Spoon about 2 tablespoons of the pumpkin cream cheese into the muffin tins over the crumb crust layer, or pour the mixture into the cake pan.

Sprinkle about 1 tablespoon of the reserved crumbs over the pumpkin filling, or on top of the cake. Spray lightly with butter-flavored cooking spray. This helps the crumbs to brown nicely. Be careful when spraying—don't hold the can too close to the crumbs or you will blow them all over your kitchen.

Bake for 20 to 25 minutes for the mini cheesecakes, 35 to 40 minutes for the standard-size. Let cool in the pan to room temperature, then chill in the refrigerator at least 2½ hours or overnight.

AUTUMN CHEESECAKE

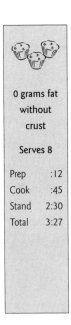

0 grams fat
without
crust

Serves 8

Prep   :12
Cook   :45
Stand   2:30
Total   3:27

If serving this during the holidays, you may want to add a stick of cinnamon and a long-stemmed cherry for garnish.

3 (8-ounce) packages fat-free cream cheese, brick type
⅔ cup granulated sugar
¾ cup canned pumpkin-pie mix
1 teaspoon vanilla extract
¾ cup egg substitute
1 (9-inch) graham cracker crust

Preheat the oven to 350 degrees.

With a wire whisk, carefully stir the cream cheese and sugar together until blended. (Don't get crazy with the whisk or you will break down the cream cheese.) Add the pumpkin pie mix and vanilla. Taste to see if you would like a tiny bit more ground cloves or cinnamon or nutmeg. If so, add a dash and continue to mix. Add the egg substitute, continue to mix until blended.

Pour very carefully into the graham cracker crust. Bake for 45 to 50 minutes or until a knife inserted in the center comes out clean.

Let cool completely on a rack and refrigerate for at least 2½ hours or overnight. Serve with fat-free whipped topping if desired.

LEMONLICIOUS CHEESECAKE

I envelope unflavored gelatin
¼ cup cold water
3 (8-ounce) packages fat-free cream cheese, at room temperature
¾ cup granulated sugar
I cup fat-free sour cream, at room temperature
I tablespoon freshly grated lemon peel
Juice from I lemon (about ½ to ⅔ cup)
¼ cup blanched almonds
I cup fresh strawberries or raspberries
I cup fresh blueberries or blackberries
I lemon slice for garnish
Fresh mint leaves for garnish

Less than 2 grams fat per serving

Serves 8

Prep	:25
Cook	:03
Stand	4:00
Total	4:28

Lightly coat an 8-inch springform pan with vegetable oil cooking spray. Set aside.

Combine the gelatin and cold water in a small saucepan. Stir, then let stand for 1 minute to soften. Place over low heat and cook, stirring, until thickened and clear, 2 or 3 minutes. Remove from the heat.

In a large mixing bowl, combine the cream cheese, sour cream, and sugar. Stir with a wire whisk until smooth (don't whip it too long or the cheese will get too thin and you will be the one crying). Beat in the dissolved gelatin, the lemon peel, and lemon juice.

Pour the mixture into the prepared pan, cover tightly with plastic wrap, and refrigerate at least 4 hours, until firm, or up to 2 days.

Toast the almonds: Place the nuts in a small heavy skillet and stir over medium heat for 2 or 3 minutes or until toasty brown. Be careful not to scorch.

Three or four hours before serving time, run a thin knife around the edge of the cheesecake to loosen it from the pan. Remove pan sides.

Arrange the berries in a decorative manner on top—maybe a circle of red, circle of blue, or triangles of each. Be creative. Have fun while thinning down. Press the toasted almonds around the sides. You can also make a design with these, and sprinkle some over the top. I usually chop the ones I am going to use on the top; that way, everyone gets a taste.

Stand the lemon slice up on top in a figure 8: Cut through the rind on opposite sides, then criss-cross cut from inside the rind to inside the rind on the opposite side. This will let you stand the slice up in a figure 8 form. Place the mint leaves on each side to garnish. Yummy!

Cookies
and
Bars

CINNAMON SUGAR DROP COOKIES

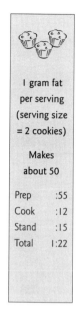

2½ cups all-purpose flour
½ teaspoon baking soda
1 teaspoon salt
¼ cup egg substitute, slightly beaten
2 tablespoons white vinegar
1½ teaspoons grated lemon rind
1 teaspoon vanilla extract
1 tablespoon butter-flavored shortening
½ cup applesauce
¼ cup (4 tablespoons) reduced-fat margarine, at room temperature
¼ cup solid-type fat-free margarine, at room temperature
1 cup sugar, plus additional for garnish
Ground cinnamon for garnish

1 gram fat per serving (serving size = 2 cookies)	
Makes about 50	
Prep	:55
Cook	:12
Stand	:15
Total	1:22

Preheat the oven to 400 degrees. Have ready 1 or 2 un-greased cookie sheets.

Combine the flour, baking soda, and salt in a bowl. Blend with a wire whisk; set aside.

In a separate bowl, combine the egg substitute, vinegar, lemon rind, and vanilla.

In a larger bowl, cream both margarines, the butter-flavored shortening, and the applesauce with an electric mixer until smooth. Add the cup of sugar gradually, creaming well.

Start adding dry ingredients to the sugar mixture alternating with egg mixture, a little at a time, blending well after each addition.

Drop by teaspoonfuls 2 inches apart onto an ungreased baking sheet; flatten with a floured fork. Sprinkle with a mixture of ½ cup sugar and 2 teaspoons of cinnamon.

Bake for 10 to 12 minutes or until lightly browned. If you like a soft cookie bake for a shorter time; if you like crispier cookies bake the full 12 minutes. Let cool completely and store in an airtight container or in the freezer until ready to serve.

MERINGUE COOKIES

Trace of fat

Serves 12

Prep   :15
Cook   :45
Stand   8:00
Total   9:00

This is not a recipe you would like to do on one of those cold damp rainy days when you're staying home and have the urge to bake. Choose a nice dry beautiful day, or make these after dinner, bake them, and leave in the oven to dry until morning, turning the oven off when the baking is finished of course.

3 egg whites, at room temperature
½ cup granulated sugar
1 teaspoon cream of tartar
1 teaspoon vanilla extract
¼ teaspoon flavoring (this may be your choice of flavors), such as almond extract

Preheat the oven to 275 degrees. Line your cookie sheet with baking parchment or—if you're like I am and live in a Gore, America, population 670 with one grocery store—you may choose to line your cookie sheet with aluminum foil. Even better, you can cut a brown paper bag or use brown package wrapping paper. Set aside.

Use a large mixing bowl, glass if possible, washed and dried. Beat the room-temperature egg whites with a hand-held mixer until soft peaks form. Start sprinkling in the sugar and cream of tartar, beating all the time, until all the sugar is mixed in well. Add vanilla and whatever other extract or flavoring you are using. Beat on high speed until the meringue is glossy and forms stiff peaks when the beater is withdrawn.

Drop by rounded teaspoonfuls 2 inches apart on the prepared baking sheet. Bake for 45 minutes. Turn off the oven and let cool completely in the oven *without opening the door.* Leaving them overnight in the turned-off oven is a great way to do these ahead. Peel the meringues from the foil, loosening them with a spatula if necessary. Store in an airtight container.

Note: If you choose chocolate extract, add about 2 tablespoons cocoa. If you choose almond extract, place a couple of tablespoons of toasted almonds in the blender or food processor and chop very fine. Fold the cocoa or nuts into the meringue before dropping onto cookie sheet.

Variation:

> *These can be smoothed on top or you can make an indentation in the middle of each and use like an edible serving dish to serve fat-free ice cream or fruit.*

OATMEAL COOKIES

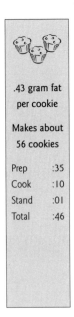

.43 gram fat
per cookie

Makes about
56 cookies

Prep	:35
Cook	:10
Stand	:01
Total	:46

1½ cups granulated sugar
½ cup firmly packed brown sugar
½ cup solid-type fat-free margarine
½ stick (4 tablespoons) light margarine
¼ cup applesauce
1 teaspoon vanilla extract
½ cup egg substitute
1½ cups all-purpose flour
1 teaspoon baking soda
¾ teaspoon ground cinnamon
¼ teaspoon salt (optional)
2½ cups quick-cooking rolled oats

Preheat the oven to 350 degrees. Lightly spray one or more baking sheets with vegetable oil cooking spray.

In a large mixing bowl, combine and cream together both sugars and both margarines. Add the applesauce and vanilla and beat with an electric mixer until light and fluffy. Blend in the egg substitute.

In a separate container, combine the flour, baking soda, cinnamon, and salt. Start adding to the sugar and margarine mixture small portions at a time. Stir in the oats.

Drop by teaspoonfuls 2 inches apart onto prepared baking sheet. Bake for 8 to 10 minutes or until lightly browned. Cool 1 minute before removing from the baking sheet to a wire cooling rack.

For crisper cookies, bake a minute or two longer; for chewier cookies, bake a minute or two less.

Store in airtight containers. Freeze cookies until needed if baking ahead; the lower-fat cookies are harder to keep fresh tasting than fat-full cookies.

LOW-FAT OATMEAL COOKIES

A nice cakelike cookie.

2 cups all-purpose flour
1 teaspoon baking soda
½ teaspoon baking powder
1 teaspoon ground cinnamon
¼ teaspoon salt (optional)
1 cup granulated sugar
⅔ cup packed brown sugar
1 cup egg substitute
⅓ cup applesauce
½ cup dark or light corn syrup, or honey
1 teaspoon vanilla extract
1¾ cups rolled oats
½ to ¾ cup raisins (optional)
¼ cup low-fat chocolate chips (optional)
¼ cup finely chopped nuts (optional)
½ cup chopped dried apricots (optional)

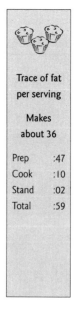

Trace of fat
per serving

Makes
about 36

Prep	:47
Cook	:10
Stand	:02
Total	:59

Preheat the oven to 375 degrees. Lightly spray one or more cookie sheets with vegetable oil cooking spray.

In a small bowl, mix the flour, soda, baking powder, cinnamon, and salt. Whisk to combine.

In a large mixing bowl, combine the granulated and brown sugars, egg substitute, applesauce, and syrup. Beat with an electric mixer until foamy. Add vanilla; mix well.

Gradually add the dry mixture to the egg mixture, stirring until well blended. This dough is stiff, so have a strong utensil.

Fold in the oats and any of the options that you choose to add at this time. When well blended, drop by tablespoonfuls about 3 inches apart on the prepared baking sheet.

Bake for 8 to 10 minutes or until lightly browned. Let stand about 2 minutes before removing with a spatula to a wire rack. Store in an airtight container or freeze for freshness.

PINEAPPLE OATMEAL DROP COOKIES

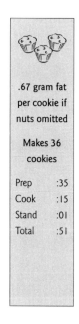

.67 gram fat per cookie if nuts omitted

Makes 36 cookies

Prep	:35
Cook	:15
Stand	:01
Total	:51

½ stick (4 tablespoons) reduced-fat margarine,
    at room temperature
¼ cup solid-type fat-free margarine, at room temperature
1 cup granulated sugar
¼ teaspoon ground cinnamon
⅛ teaspoon ground nutmeg
¼ cup egg substitute
1 (8-ounce) can crushed pineapple, undrained
1 cup all-purpose flour
½ teaspoon salt
½ teaspoon baking soda
1½ cups rolled oats
¼ cup chopped nuts (optional)

Preheat the oven to 375 degrees. Lightly coat one or more baking sheets with vegetable oil cooking spray.

Cream together the margarines and sugar; stir in cinnamon and nutmeg. Beat in the egg substitute. Stir in the pineapple, then add the flour mixed with salt and baking soda. Stir until well blended.

Add the rolled oats and nuts if using. Mix well. Drop by teaspoonfuls onto the prepared baking sheets, spacing the cookies 2 inches apart.

Bake for 12 to 15 minutes, until lightly browned. Let cool for one minute in the pan before moving to a wire rack to cool completely.

GRANDMA ROHDE'S COOKIES

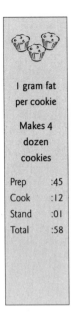

I gram fat per cookie

Makes 4 dozen cookies

Prep	:45
Cook	:12
Stand	:01
Total	:58

This is a large recipe, I don't make cookies very often, but when I do, there are enough to have some for the grandkids after Bob samples.

1¾ cups granulated sugar
2 cups packed brown sugar
⅓ cup (5⅓ tablespoons) light margarine
⅓ cup solid-type fat-free margarine
⅔ cup applesauce
1½ teaspoons vanilla extract
1 cup egg substitute
3¾ cups all-purpose flour
2 teaspoons baking soda
1 teaspoon baking powder
½ cup shredded sweetened dried coconut
½ cup miniature chocolate chips
¼ cup chopped nuts (optional)
8 cups Rice Krispies cereal

Preheat the oven to 350 degrees. Have ready one or more ungreased baking sheets.

In a large mixing bowl, combine the granulated and brown sugars, margarines, and applesauce. Beat with an electric mixer until fluffy. Add the vanilla and egg substitute; mix well.

In a separate bowl, whisk the flour, soda, and baking powder together; start adding slowly to the sugar mixture. When well blended, add the coconut, chocolate chips, and nuts if desired. Fold in the Rice Krispies.

Drop by rounded tablespoonfuls spaced 3 inches apart on the baking sheets. Bake 8 to 12 minutes or until lightly golden brown. *Do not overbake!*

Cool 1 minute in pans before removing with a spatula to a wire rack. Let cool completely on the rack.

APPLESAUCE COOKIES

2 cups all-purpose flour

1 teaspoon ground cinnamon

½ teaspoon ground nutmeg

¼ teaspoon ground cloves

¼ teaspoon salt

½ teaspoon baking soda

1 teaspoon baking powder

¼ cup (4 tablespoons) reduced-fat margarine

¼ cup solid-type fat-free margarine

¾ cup honey

¼ cup egg substitute

1 cup thick applesauce

¼ cup chopped nuts (optional)

.37 gram fat
per cookie

Makes 3
dozen
cookies

Prep	:35
Cook	:12
Stand	:16
Total	1:03

Preheat the oven to 375 degrees. Lightly coat one or more cookie sheets with vegetable oil cooking spray.

In a mixing bowl, combine the flour, cinnamon, nutmeg, cloves, salt, baking soda, and baking powder. Mix thoroughly with a wire whisk.

In a large bowl with an electric mixer, cream the margarines and honey together. Add the egg substitute and beat well.

Add the flour mixture and the applesauce alternately to the margarine mixture, beginning and ending with flour. Beat well after each addition.

Fold in the nuts if using. Drop by teaspoonfuls onto the prepared baking sheets, spacing the cookies 2 inches apart.

Bake for 10 to 12 minutes, or until the edges are lightly browned. Let stand for 1 minute, then remove the cookies with a spatula to cool on a wire rack. Store in an airtight container after completely cool.

DATE COOKIES

.67 gram fat
per cookie

Makes about
36 cookies

Prep   :25
Cook   :15
Stand   :16
Total   :56

¼ cup solid-type fat-free margarine, at room temperature
¼ cup (4 tablespoons) lower-fat margarine, at room temperature
¾ cup packed brown sugar
¼ cup egg substitute
½ teaspoon vanilla extract
2 cups all-purpose flour
2 teaspoons baking powder
¼ teaspoon salt
¼ cup fat-free milk
½ cup chopped dates

Preheat the oven to 350 degrees. Lightly coat one or more cookie sheets with vegetable oil cooking spray.

Combine the margarines and brown sugar in a large bowl and beat with an electric mixer until fluffy. Add the egg substitute and vanilla; mix thoroughly.

In a small bowl, whisk together the flour, baking powder, and salt. Stir into the margarine mixture with the milk. When thoroughly combined, fold in the dates.

Drop by teaspoonfuls onto the prepared pan, spacing the cookies 2 inches apart, and bake for 12 to 15 minutes or until lightly browned. Cool in the pan for 1 minute, then transfer to a wire rack and cool completely.

GERMAN CHOCOLATE DROP COOKIES

2 (4-ounce) bars German sweet chocolate
1 tablespoon lower-in-fat margarine
¼ cup egg substitute
¾ cup granulated sugar
½ teaspoon vanilla extract
½ cup all-purpose flour
¼ teaspoon baking powder
¼ teaspoon ground cinnamon
⅛ teaspoon salt (optional)
¼ cup chopped nuts (optional)

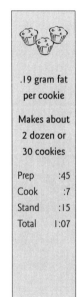

.19 gram fat
per cookie

Makes about
2 dozen or
30 cookies

Prep	:45
Cook	:7
Stand	:15
Total	1:07

Preheat the oven to 350 degrees. Lightly coat a cookie sheet with vegetable oil cooking spray.

In the top part of a double boiler over simmering water, melt the chocolate together with the margarine. Stir; set aside to cool.

In a large bowl, beat the egg substitute with an electric mixer until foamy. Beat in the sugar, 2 tablespoons at a time. Continue to beat at medium speed until thickened, about 5 minutes. Blend in the chocolate and the vanilla extract.

Whisk together in a separate bowl the flour, baking powder, cinnamon, and salt. Stir into the chocolate mixture. Fold in the nuts if using.

Drop the dough by teaspoonfuls onto the prepared baking sheet, spacing the cookies 2 inches apart. Bake for 8 to 10 minutes, or until the cookies feel set when very lightly touched.

Cool in the pan for 1 minute, then transfer to a wire rack and cool completely.

CHOCOLATE CHIP COOKIES

1.5 grams fat
per cookie

Makes about
2 dozen
cookies

Prep   :25
Cook   :08
Stand   :01
Total   :34

¼ cup (4 tablespoons) reduced-fat margarine, at room temperature
⅔ cup packed brown sugar
½ teaspoon vanilla extract
¼ cup egg substitute
1 cup plus 2 tablespoons all-purpose flour
½ teaspoon baking soda
Pinch of salt
½ cup reduced-fat chocolate chips

Preheat the oven to 375 degrees.

In a large mixing bowl, with an electric mixer, beat the margarine and brown sugar together until light and fluffy. Add the vanilla and egg substitute; mix again.

Combine the flour, baking soda, and salt. Begin adding the flour mixture to the egg mixture, small amounts at a time. When well blended and a nicely textured dough, fold in the chocolate chips.

Drop by rounded teaspoonfuls about 2 inches apart onto an ungreased cookie sheet. Bake for 7 to 8 minutes. *Do not overbake.* Cool 1 minute, then remove from the baking sheet to a wire rack and cool completely.

Store in an airtight container or freeze as soon as possible.

QUICK CHOCOLATE CHIP COOKIES

Now you can have your cookie and eat it too, and it is quick and easy when taking out the fat from a convenient mix.

1 package chocolate chip cookie mix (bag type)
¼ cup (4 tablespoons) light margarine, at room temperature
¾ cup applesauce
½ cup egg substitute

Preheat the oven to 350 degrees.

Empty the contents of the package into a mixing bowl. Add the margarine and applesauce. Start stirring with a wooden spoon; add the egg substitute. When mixed well, drop the dough by spoonfuls onto an ungreased baking sheet, spacing the cookies 2 inches apart.

Bake for about 9 to 11 minutes. These will be soft cookies due to the fact that we did not add any fat. They are de-

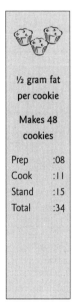

½ gram fat
per cookie

Makes 48
cookies

Prep	:08
Cook	:11
Stand	:15
Total	:34

licious. Store in an airtight bag or container or freeze until ready for use.

SNAP, CRACKLE & POP COOKIES

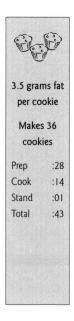

3.5 grams fat
per cookie

Makes 36
cookies

Prep	:28
Cook	:14
Stand	:01
Total	:43

¼ cup (4 tablespoons) reduced-fat margarine,
    at room temperature
¼ cup (4 tablespoons) solid-type fat-free margarine,
    at room temperature
1 cup granulated sugar
1 cup powdered sugar, plus additional 1 cup for coating
½ cup applesauce
½ cup egg substitute
1 teaspoon vanilla extract
5 cups all-purpose flour
1 teaspoon baking soda
1 teaspoon cream of tartar
1 cup Rice Krispies cereal
2 tablespoons chocolate chips

Preheat the oven to 350 degrees. Lightly coat a cookie sheet or jelly roll pan with vegetable oil cooking spray.

In a medium-size mixing bowl, combine both margarines and beat until fluffy. Beat in the granulated sugar and 1 cup of powdered sugar. Add the applesauce, egg substitute, and vanilla; continue beating until blended.

In a large mixing bowl, combine the flour with the baking soda and cream of tartar. Whisk until thoroughly mixed. Add to the sugar-egg mixture and beat until well blended. Fold in the cereal and chocolate chips.

Drop by large spoonfuls onto the prepared baking sheet, spacing the cookies 2 inches apart. Bake 12 to 14 minutes. Let stand for 1 minute. Roll the cookies in powdered sugar while still warm. Finish cooling on a rack.

Variation:

> *The dough can be spread in a fairly thin layer on a baking sheet and cut into squares after baking. It is also excellent as a crust.*

LIGHT MAGIC BARS

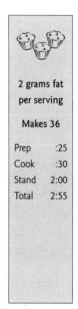

2 grams fat
per serving

Makes 36

Prep	:25
Cook	:30
Stand	2:00
Total	2:55

¼ cup (4 tablespoons) reduced-fat margarine,
  at room temperature
¼ cup solid-type fat-free margarine, at room temperature
1½ cups low-fat graham cracker crumbs
  (about 20 cracker squares)
1 (14-ounce) can fat-free sweetened condensed milk
  (*not* evaporated milk)
6 ounces reduced-fat chocolate chips
1 cup flaked coconut (3 grams fat per 2 tablespoons)
¼ cup chopped nuts (optional)

Preheat the oven to 325 degrees. Place both margarines in an 11 x 7 x 1½-inch glass baking dish and melt in the oven (or melt in the microwave). Stir to blend the two together and spread evenly over the bottom of the dish.

Pour the graham cracker crumbs evenly over the melted margarine.

Pour the condensed milk over the crumbs.

Mix the chocolate chips, coconut, and nuts if using. Sprinkle evenly over the condensed milk layer, pressing down until the mixture is lightly packed.

Bake for 25 to 30 minutes or until lightly browned. Let cool completely in the baking dish; cut into 36 bars. Store loosely covered at room temperature.

TRIPLE CHOCOLATE BROWNIES

7 grams fat
entire
dessert

Makes 12

Prep   :25
Cook   :30
Stand   :30
Total   1:25

This is really chocolatey.

1 box reduced-fat fudge brownie mix
½ teaspoon ground cinnamon
1 tablespoon instant coffee granules
1 tablespoon hot water or coffee
1 tablespoon coconut amaretto
⅔ cup applesauce
¼ cup egg substitute
½ cup sauerkraut, rinsed of brine and drained
2 tablespoons reduced-fat chocolate chips

GLAZE:

⅔ cup powdered sugar
1 teaspoon instant coffee granules
1 tablespoon unsweetened cocoa powder
Pinch of ground cinnamon
1 tablespoon fat-free milk or hot coffee
1 teaspoon coconut amaretto

Preheat the oven to 325 degrees. Lightly coat the bottom of an 11 x 7 x 1½-inch baking dish with vegetable oil cooking spray.

In a mixing bowl, combine the brownie mix and the ½ teaspoon of cinnamon.

In a separate small bowl, dissolve the coffee granules in the hot water and mix in the amaretto, applesauce, and egg substitute. Add to the brownie mixture and stir just until moistened. Stir in the kraut and the chocolate chips.

Pour the batter into the prepared pan. Bake for 30 minutes or just until the edges are firm—do not overbake. Let cool in the baking dish on a rack.

Make the glaze: Combine the powdered sugar, coffee granules, cocoa, and cinnamon in a small bowl. Stir in the milk and amaretto.

Pour the glaze over the cooled brownies, spreading to the edges to cover. To serve, cut into squares.

PUMPKIN BARS

I gram fat
per serving if
prepared
with crust
and topping

Makes 12

Prep   :20
Cook   :35
Stand   :45
Total   1:40

1 recipe Crust and Topping for Dessert Bars (see page 153)
⅓ cup packed brown sugar
⅓ cup granulated sugar
1 teaspoon all-purpose flour
⅛ teaspoon ground cloves
¼ teaspoon ground nutmeg
½ teaspoon ground cinnamon
¼ cup egg substitute
1 (14-ounce) can fat-free sweetened condensed milk
   (*not* evaporated milk)
1 cup canned solid-pack pumpkin

Preheat the oven to 375 degrees. Make the crust and topping according to recipe directions. Set the topping mixture aside. Press the crust mixture evenly over the bottom of an 11 x 7 x 1½-inch glass baking dish and bake for 10 minutes.

In a large mixing bowl, combine the brown sugar, granulated sugar, and flour. Mix with a wire whisk. Add the cloves, nutmeg, and cinnamon and continue to mix. When well blended, stir in the egg substitute, condensed milk, and pumpkin.

When the mixture is smooth, pour it into the prepared crust. Crumble the reserved topping mixture evenly on top. Lower the heat to 350 degrees and bake for 30 to 35 minutes or until a knife inserted into the center comes out clean.

Let cool in the pan on a rack. To serve, cut into bars. Garnish with fat-free ice cream or whipped topping if desired.

LEMON SQUARES

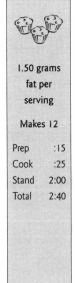

1 prebaked bar crust (see recipes on page 154)
3 egg whites
1 cup granulated sugar
¼ cup egg substitute
¼ cup applesauce
1 teaspoon lemon zest (grated lemon peel)
¼ cup lemon juice
3 tablespoons all-purpose flour
½ teaspoon baking powder

1.50 grams
fat per
serving

Makes 12

Prep   :15
Cook   :25
Stand   2:00
Total   2:40

Prepare and bake the crust according to recipe directions. Leave the oven turned on to 350 degrees.

In a glass bowl very clean of any grease, whip the egg whites along with the sugar and egg substitute until the mixture starts to thicken and is nice and foamy. Add the applesauce, lemon zest, juice, flour, and baking powder. Continue beating until well blended and smooth.

Pour the filling over the warm crust. Continue to bake for an additional 20 to 25 minutes or until a knife inserted into the center comes out clean and the top is lightly browned.

Let cool completely on wire rack. Cut into squares.

APPLE SQUARES

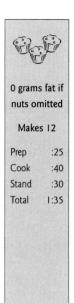

0 grams fat if
nuts omitted

Makes 12

Prep	:25
Cook	:40
Stand	:30
Total	1:35

I cup all-purpose flour

½ cup granulated sugar

I teaspoon baking powder

Pinch of salt

¼ teaspoon ground nutmeg

⅔ cup fat-free milk

¼ cup egg substitute

3 medium apples (about 3 cups peeled, cored, and chopped)

¼ cup raisins or dried cranberries (optional)

¼ cup finely chopped nuts (optional)

¼ cup packed brown sugar

½ teaspoon ground cinnamon

Preheat the oven to 350 degrees. Prepare a 13 x 9 x 2-inch baking dish by spraying lightly with vegetable oil cooking spray.

Combine the flour, granulated sugar, baking powder, salt, and nutmeg in a mixing bowl. Blend well. Beat in the milk and egg substitute. Spoon into the prepared pan, spreading evenly. Evenly layer the apples, raisins or cranberries, and nuts over the batter.

In a small bowl, combine the brown sugar and cinnamon; sprinkle over all. Bake uncovered for 30 to 40 minutes or until the apples are tender and lightly browned. Let cool in the pan on a rack. Serve warm or cold, cut into squares.

APPLE-TOPPED DESSERT BARS

These are cakelike but they are also brownielike. You may frost if desired. I just sprinkle powdered sugar over them and poof! they're gone!

0 grams fat

Makes 36

Prep	:50
Cook	:45
Stand	:40
Total	2:15

2¾ cups all-purpose flour

½ teaspoon baking soda

½ teaspoon baking powder

1½ teaspoons ground cinnamon

½ cup applesauce

3 tablespoons fat-free margarine

¾ cup egg substitute

¾ cup packed brown sugar

1 cup granulated sugar

1½ teaspoons vanilla extract

1 (21-ounce) can apple slices, unsweetened

½ cup raisins (optional)

¼ cup chopped nuts (optional—bars will not be fat-free if added)

Preheat the oven to 350 degrees. Coat a jelly roll pan lightly with vegetable oil cooking spray.

Combine in a bowl the flour, soda, baking powder, and cinnamon.

In a separate large mixing bowl, blend the applesauce, margarine, egg substitute, brown sugar, granulated sugar, and vanilla. Mix until well blended.

Gradually add the flour mixture to the applesauce mixture, beating just until moistened. Stir in the apples, and the raisins and nuts, if using. Continue to mix with a spoon until well blended.

Pour into the prepared pan, spreading with a spatula until evenly distributed.

Bake for 40 to 45 minutes, until knife comes out clean when inserted into the center. Let cool completely; cut into bars.

CHERRY SQUARES

¾ gram fat
per bar

Makes 8

Prep	:15
Cook	:30
Stand	2:00
Total	2:45

1 recipe Oat Crust (page 154)
1 (8-ounce) package fat-free cream cheese, softened
⅓ cup granulated sugar
¼ cup egg substitute
1 (21-ounce) can cherry pie filling

Prepare and bake the crust according to recipe directions. Turn the oven heat down to 350 degrees.

In a medium-size mixing bowl, combine the cream cheese and sugar, stirring carefully with a wire whisk so the cream cheese does not break down. Add the egg substitute. Blend. Pour over the prepared crust.

Bake for 15 minutes, remove from the oven, and spread cherry pie filling over the cream cheese mixture. Return to the oven and continue baking for 15 additional minutes.

Remove to a rack and let cool completely. Chill before cutting into squares for serving.

PINEAPPLE BARS I

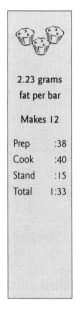

1½ cups all-purpose flour
1 teaspoon baking powder
½ teaspoon baking soda
⅛ teaspoon salt (optional)
¼ cup (4 tablespoons) lower-fat margarine, at room temperature
¼ cup (4 tablespoons) fat-free margarine, at room temperature
2 cups granulated sugar
1 cup egg substitute
1 (9-ounce) can crushed pineapple, drained
Powdered sugar for garnish

2.23 grams
fat per bar

Makes 12

Prep	:38
Cook	:40
Stand	:15
Total	1:33

Preheat the oven to 350 degrees. Lightly spray an 11 x 7 x 1½-inch baking pan with vegetable oil cooking spray. Lightly dust with flour; shake out any excess.

Mix together the flour, baking powder, baking soda, and salt in a small bowl.

In a large bowl with an electric mixer, combine the 2 margarines and beat until light in color, about 3 minutes. Add the sugar in a steady stream while continuing to beat for 3 or 4 minutes. Beat in the egg substitute ¼ cup at a time.

Fold in half the flour mixture with a large rubber spatula, then fold in half the drained pineapple. Fold in the remaining flour, then the remaining pineapple.

Pour the batter into the prepared pan and bake for 35 to 40 minutes or until a wooden pick inserted in the center of the cake comes out clean.

(recipe continues)

Let cool in the pan on a rack for about 15 minutes, then sprinkle with powdered sugar. When completely cool, cut into bars.

PINEAPPLE BARS II

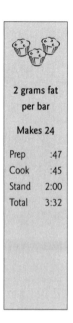

2 grams fat
per bar

Makes 24

Prep   :47
Cook   :45
Stand   2:00
Total   3:32

CRUMB CRUST:

1½ cups all-purpose flour
1 cup rolled oats
1 cup packed brown sugar
Pinch of salt
½ stick (4 tablespoons) reduced-fat margarine
½ cup solid-type fat-free margarine
¼ cup chopped nuts (optional)

FILLING:

2 tablespoons packed brown sugar
1 (8-ounce) can crushed pineapple, undrained
1 teaspoon cornstarch dissolved in 1 tablespoon cold water

Preheat the oven to 350 degrees. Coat a 12 x 8 x 2-inch baking dish with vegetable oil cooking spray.

Make the crust: In a mixing bowl, combine the flour, oats, brown sugar, and salt. Using a pastry blender or 2 knives, cut in both margarines. Add the nuts if using.

Reserve 2 cups of the crumb mixture. Press the remainder evenly over the bottom of the prepared baking dish.

Make the filling: In a medium saucepan, combine the brown sugar and pineapple. Bring to a boil, add the cornstarch, and simmer while stirring for 4 or 5 minutes or until thickened and clear.

Spoon the pineapple mixture into the prepared pan and top with the reserved crumbs. Pat lightly. Bake for 35 to 45 minutes or until nicely browned. Let cool on a rack. When cooled completely, cut into bars.

PECAN PIE SURPRISE BARS

CRUST:

1 (18¼-ounce) package reduced-fat cake mix (white or yellow)
¼ cup (4 tablespoons) reduced-fat margarine, at room temperature
½ cup applesauce
¼ cup egg substitute

FILLING:

⅔ cup reserved cake mix
½ cup packed brown sugar
1½ cups dark corn syrup (I prefer waffle syrup with a maple flavor)
1 teaspoon vanilla extract
¾ cup egg substitute
¼ cup chopped pecans (optional) or nutlike cereal

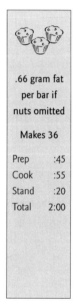

.66 gram fat
per bar if
nuts omitted

Makes 36

Prep	:45
Cook	:55
Stand	:20
Total	2:00

Preheat the oven to 350 degrees. Lightly coat the bottom and sides of a 13 x 9 x 2-inch baking pan with vegetable oil cooking spray.

Empty the package of cake mix into a large bowl. Measure out ⅔ cup and reserve for use in the filling.

Make the crust: With a pastry blender or 2 knives, cut the margarine into the bowl of cake mix until it is in pea-size pieces. Add the applesauce and egg substitute and mix with a fork until moistened and crumbly. Press in the bottom and partly up the sides of the prepared pan. Bake for 15 to 20 minutes or until golden brown.

While the crust is baking, prepare the filling: In a bowl with an electric mixer, combine the reserved cake mix with the brown sugar, syrup, vanilla, and egg substitute. Beat on medium speed until blended.

Remove the partially baked crust from the oven and pour the filling over the hot crust. Sprinkle with nuts if using. Return to the oven and bake about 35 minutes longer, until a knife inserted in the center comes out clean. Let cool for 20 to 30 minutes. Cut into 36 squares and serve warm.

CRUST AND TOPPING FOR DESSERT BARS

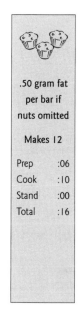

CRUST:

1⅓ cups rolled oats

1 tablespoon nutlike cereal, such as Grape-Nuts

¼ cup finely chopped nuts (optional)

½ cup flour

¾ cup packed brown sugar

¼ teaspoon baking powder

¼ cup applesauce

1 tablespoon light margarine, melted

TOPPING:

⅔ cup rolled oats

1 tablespoon all-purpose flour

2 tablespoons packed brown sugar

2 tablespoons nutlike cereal

½ tablespoon light margarine, melted

1 tablespoon applesauce

.50 gram fat
per bar if
nuts omitted

Makes 12

Prep	:06
Cook	:10
Stand	:00
Total	:16

For the crust: Combine the oats, cereal, flour, brown sugar, nuts (if using), and baking powder in a mixing bowl. Blend well. Add the applesauce and melted margarine. Mix with a fork just until moistened and crumbly. To partially bake, press in the bottom of an oiled 11 x 7-inch baking dish. Bake at 375 degrees for 10 minutes.

For the topping: In a mixing bowl, combine the oats, flour, brown sugar, and cereal. Mix well. Add the margarine and applesauce. Mix until crumbly. Bake as directed in recipe.

CRUST FOR DESSERT BARS

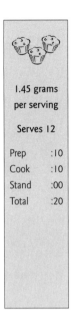

1.45 grams
per serving

Serves 12

Prep	:10
Cook	:10
Stand	:00
Total	:20

1 cup all-purpose flour
½ cup powdered sugar
¼ cup applesauce
2 tablespoons light margarine, melted

Preheat oven to 375 degrees.

Combine in a small mixing bowl the flour and sugar. Mix to blend. Pour in the applesauce mixed with the melted margarine; stir with a fork until crumbly.

To partially bake, press the mixture on the bottom of an 11 x 7-inch baking pan. Bake for 10 minutes, remove from the oven, add the filling of your choice, and bake according to recipe directions.

OAT CRUST

.50 grams fat
per serving

Serves 8

Prep	:05
Cook	:15
Stand	:00
Total	:20

1½ cups rolled oats
⅓ cup pourable fat-free margarine
¾ cup sugar

Preheat oven to 400 degrees.

Combine the oats, margarine, and sugar. Mix well. Press into the bottom of an 8-inch square baking pan lightly sprayed with cooking spray. Bake for 15 minutes.

CHOCOLATE GOODIE BARS

1¾ cups all-purpose flour
1½ cups powdered sugar
½ cup unsweetened cocoa powder
¼ cup solid-type fat-free margarine, chilled
4 tablespoons (½ stick) fat-reduced margarine, chilled
½ cup applesauce, chilled
1 (8-ounce) package fat-free cream cheese, at room temperature
1 (14-ounce) fat-free sweetened condensed milk (*not* evaporated milk)
¼ cup egg substitute
2 teaspoons vanilla extract
¼ cup chopped walnuts (optional)

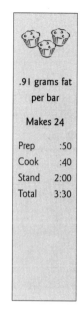

.91 grams fat per bar

Makes 24

Prep	:50
Cook	:40
Stand	2:00
Total	3:30

Preheat the oven to 350 degrees. Coat the bottom of a 13 x 9 x 2-inch baking pan with vegetable oil cooking spray.

In a blender or food processor, combine the flour, sugar, cocoa, both margarines, and applesauce. Pulse to blend until the mixture resembles coarse crumbs.

Measure out and reserve 2 cups of the crumb mixture for the topping. Pour the remainder into the prepared baking pan and press evenly over the bottom. Bake for 15 minutes.

While the crust is baking, put the cream cheese in a large bowl and stir gently with a wire whisk. Gradually add the condensed milk, stirring until smooth. Mix in the egg substitute and vanilla and stir until well blended.

Remove the crust from the oven and pour the cream cheese mixture over the hot crust. Combine the nuts (if using) and the reserved crumbs. Sprinkle evenly over the cheese mixture. Bake for 25 minutes or until bubbly.

Remove to a rack and let cool completely. Refrigerate. Cut into bars to serve. Store covered in the refrigerator.

COOKIE PIZZA

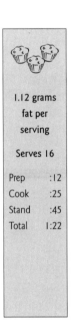

1.12 grams
fat per
serving

Serves 16

Prep	:12
Cook	:25
Stand	:45
Total	1:22

½ stick (4 tablespoons) reduced-fat margarine, at room temperature
½ cup solid-type fat-free margarine, at room temperature
¾ cup sugar
¼ cup egg substitute
1 teaspoon vanilla extract
1½ cups all-purpose flour
1 (8-ounce) package fat-free strawberry-flavored cream cheese
2 medium bananas, sliced thin
¼ cup strawberry, pineapple, or chocolate ice cream topping
¼ cup chopped maraschino cherries
¼ cup finely chopped nuts (optional)

Preheat the oven to 350 degrees. Lightly coat a 12-inch pizza pan with vegetable oil cooking spray.

Combine the 2 margarines in a mixing bowl and beat until creamy. Add the sugar, continuing to beat until very fluffy and well blended. Stir in the egg substitute and vanilla and mix until smooth. Gradually stir in the flour, mixing with a wooden spoon until thoroughly blended.

Spread the dough evenly in the prepared pan. Bake for 20 to 25 minutes or until light golden brown. Let cool completely in the pan on a wire rack.

Just before serving, spread the cookie evenly with the cream cheese. Arrange the banana slices on top. Drizzle ice cream topping over the bananas; you may choose to use 1 or all 3 flavors. Sprinkle cherries and nuts over all. To serve, cut into pie-shaped wedges. Refrigerate any leftovers.

CHOCOLATE CHERRY PIZZA DESSERT

This may also be baked in a 13 x 9 x 2-inch pan and cut into squares to serve.

1 (20½-ounce) package low-fat brownie mix
⅔ cup water

TOPPING:

2 (21-ounce) cans cherry pie filling
½ (14-ounce) can fat-free sweetened condensed milk
    (*not* evaporated milk)
1 (12-ounce) tub fat-free frozen whipped topping, thawed
¼ cup pecans, chopped fine (optional)

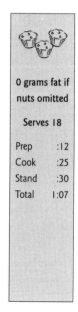

0 grams fat if
nuts omitted

Serves 18

Prep	:12
Cook	:25
Stand	:30
Total	1:07

Preheat the oven to 350 degrees. Prepare a 14-inch pizza pan by spraying with vegetable oil cooking spray.

Combine the brownie mix with ⅔ cup of water, mix well, and spread evenly onto the pan. Bake for 25 minutes or until a toothpick inserted in the center comes out clean.

While brownie mix is baking, prepare topping: In a bowl, combine ¾ can of cherry pie filling with ½ can of condensed milk. Fold in the whipped topping. When blended well, cover and refrigerate until needed.

When the brownie mix is baked, place on a wire rack to cool in the pan. Pour 1 can of cherry pie filling and the remaining filling from the other can on top of the brownies, spreading evenly. Let cool completely. When totally cooled, spread the topping over cherries. Sprinkle chopped nuts evenly over the topping. Cut into wedges, not too large, and serve as dessert pizza.

Fruit Desserts

FROZEN GRAPES

Grapes contain flavonoids that detoxify bad LDL cholesterol and fortify blood vessels. Present in red wine and red grape juice, they are known as one of the top cancer fighters. They have anticoagulant, or blood-thinning properties.

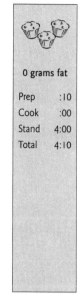

0 grams fat

Prep	:10
Cook	:00
Stand	4:00
Total	4:10

Buy red grapes when in season, or when they are on sale at your local supermarket or vegetable stand.

Wash under cold running water; lay on a kitchen towel to dry. When dry, pluck the grapes from the stems. Put in snack-size zipper-type bags. Place in the freezer for several hours.

Note: This is one of the ways I learned to eat red grapes. If you remember, I used to hate fruit.

I call these my grapesicles. They are most cooling and refreshing during very hot weather. If I am outside working in the yard, I take a cupful and munch on them while working. It keeps me from getting hungry and keeps me cooled down. You may also roll them in sugar before they dry. After they dry, lay them in a single layer to freeze, on a cookie sheet or the like. Great at parties.

CREAMY FRUIT COMPOTE

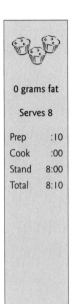

0 grams fat

Serves 8

Prep	:10
Cook	:00
Stand	8:00
Total	8:10

1 (16-ounce) can apricot halves
2 (16-ounce) cans sliced peaches
1 (16-ounce) can pineapple chunks
1 (11-ounce) can mandarin oranges
1 (10-ounce) package frozen strawberries, thawed
1 small (0.9-ounce) box instant sugar-free vanilla pudding mix

Drain all the cans of fruit in a strainer or colander set over a bowl. Save the liquid for another use. Place the fruit in a large mixing bowl. Add the thawed strawberries, juice and all.

Sprinkle the vanilla pudding over the fruit. Toss carefully to mix lightly. Pour into a pretty serving bowl. Refrigerate at least 8 hours. Sliced bananas may be added about 2 hours before serving.

GLAZED FRUIT

Very good with fat-free frozen yogurt.

Fruit of your choice: bananas, apples, fresh pineapple
1 cup firmly packed brown sugar
1 teaspoon ground cinnamon

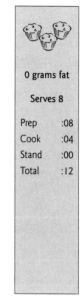

0 grams fat

Serves 8

Prep	:08
Cook	:04
Stand	:00
Total	:12

Preheat the broiler. Cover a baking sheet with foil: less mess to clean up.

Prepare the fruit. If using bananas, peel and slice lengthwise and then crosswise. If using apples, peel, core, and slice them in half-moon slices. If using fresh pineapple, peel, core, and cut into wedges.

Arrange the fruit on the baking sheet close together and in a single layer. Combine the brown sugar and cinnamon. Sprinkle over the fruit. Broil for 3 to 4 minutes or until the sugar bubbles and the fruit is nicely glazed.

LEMON FLUFF

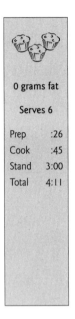

0 grams fat

Serves 6

Prep	:26
Cook	:45
Stand	3:00
Total	4:11

4 egg whites, at room temperature
I cup granulated sugar
⅓ cup all-purpose flour
½ cup egg substitute
½ cup fat-free milk
Juice of I lemon (about ⅓ cup)

Preheat the oven to 350 degrees. Spray the bottom of a 3-quart casserole or soufflé dish with butter-flavored cooking spray. Have ready a roasting pan that is large enough to hold the casserole.

In a very clean glass mixing bowl, beat the egg whites until they form stiff peaks. Set aside.

In a large separate bowl, combine the sugar and flour and blend with a wire whisk.

In another separate bowl, beat the egg substitute and add the milk and lemon juice. Add to flour mixture.

Gently fold in the stiffly beaten egg whites with a rubber spatula. Your mixture will be a little lumpy-looking, but don't beat or fold until perfectly smooth.

Pour the mixture into the prepared casserole and place the casserole in the dry roasting pan. Slip the pan into the oven and pour enough scalding-hot tap water into the roasting pan to come about halfway up the side of the casserole.

Bake for about 45 minutes, or until the custard is set but still jiggly in the center. Let cool for about an hour; refrigerate until chilled.

MERINGUE-TOPPED APPLES

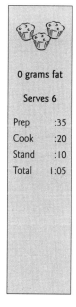

4 large cooking apples
Juice of 1 lemon or ¼ cup bottled juice
1½ cups sugar plus additional for topping
1 cup amaretto plus additional for topping
Juice and grated rind of 1 orange
3 egg whites

0 grams fat	
Serves 6	
Prep	:35
Cook	:20
Stand	:10
Total	1:05

Peel and core the apples. Cut apples into thick slices. Sprinkle slices with lemon juice to prevent browning.

In a large saucepan, combine 1 cup of the sugar, 1 cup of the amaretto, and the orange rind and juice. Heat until bubbly. Add the apple slices and simmer gently until the apples are translucent but still hold their shape.

Spoon the apples and some of their liquid into small individual custard cups (ovenproof such as Pyrex). In a very clean (no grease film), glass mixing bowl, beat the egg whites until foamy. Gradually beat in the remaining ½ cup of sugar and teaspoon of amaretto. Beat on high speed until thick and glossy.

Preheat the oven to 350 degrees at this time. Spoon the meringue over the apples in the individual dishes, being sure that it covers the apples and touches the edge all the way around.

(recipe continues)

Bake in the preheated oven for 15 to 20 minutes or until lightly browned. (I place my individual dishes on a cookie sheet to keep from tipping between the grates in the oven shelves.)

Variations:

Apples can be prepared ahead, covered, and refrigerated until time to top with meringue. They can also be topped and set into the refrigerator until time to cook and serve warm.

Sprinkle a tiny bit of cinnamon on meringue before baking for garnish.

BAKED APPLES

I gram fat
per serving
max

Serves 6

Prep	:20
Cook	:50
Stand	:30
Total	1:40

6 large apples (Rome, Golden Delicious, or your choice)
¼ cup packed brown sugar
2 tablespoons fat-free margarine
½ teaspoon ground cinnamon
Chopped walnuts (optional)
½ cup plus ¼ cup coconut amaretto
¼ cup honey
I teaspoon fresh lemon juice

Preheat the oven to 350 degrees. Spray a shallow 2-quart baking dish lightly with butter-flavored cooking spray.

Core the apples from the top, being careful not to dig a hole all the way through. Try to stop ½ inch from the bottom of the apples. Not easy, but try. Peel two or three circles around the apple, just about halfway down, leaving a bowl effect with the apple skin.

In a small bowl, mix the brown sugar, margarine, and cinnamon. You may want to add a few walnuts, but be careful of the grams you're adding. Stuff equal amounts of the sugar mixture into the center of each apple. Pour ½ cup of the amaretto over and into the apples, in equal amounts for each.

Combine the honey, lemon juice, and the reserved ¼ cup of amaretto. Drizzle over and around the apples.

Bake, basting the apples with the honey mixture from the bottom of the baking dish several times, for 45 to 50 minutes or until the apples are tender when pierced with a knife. Let cool about 30 minutes. Serve warm.

BAKED BANANAS

6 firm ripe bananas
2 tablespoons pourable fat-free margarine
2 tablespoons lemon juice
⅓ cup packed brown sugar
6 tablespoons coconut amaretto (optional, but highly
    recommended)

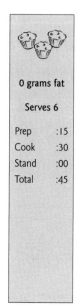

0 grams fat

Serves 6

Prep	:15
Cook	:30
Stand	:00
Total	:45

Preheat the oven to 275 degrees. Lightly coat an 11 x 9 baking dish or shallow casserole with vegetable oil cooking spray.

Peel the bananas and slice them in half lengthwise. Arrange in the baking dish in 1 layer.

Mix the margarine, lemon juice, brown sugar, and amaretto in a small bowl. Pour over the bananas. Bake uncovered for 30 minutes or until soft and pale golden. Serve hot with, if desired, fat-free ice cream or fat-free chocolate sauce.

QUICK DRESSING FOR FRUIT COMPOTE

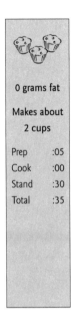

0 grams fat

Makes about
2 cups

Prep   :05
Cook   :00
Stand   :30
Total   :35

1 cup honey
6 tablespoons crushed pineapple
½ cup lemon juice

Place all 3 ingredients in a blender or food processor. Process until blended and smooth. Pour over fruit. Refrigerate until time to serve; set out for at least ½ hour before serving.

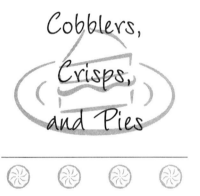

Cobblers, Crisps, and Pies

APPLE CRISP

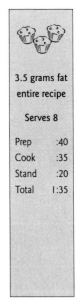

¾ cup packed brown sugar
½ cup all-purpose flour
½ cup rolled oats, dry
¾ teaspoon ground cinnamon
¾ teaspoon ground nutmeg
⅓ cup solid-type fat-free margarine
5 to 6 cooking apples, peeled, cored, and sliced (about 4 or 5 cups)
½ cup granulated sugar

3.5 grams fat entire recipe	
Serves 8	
Prep	:40
Cook	:35
Stand	:20
Total	1:35

Preheat the oven to 375 degrees. Spray a 2- or 3-quart baking dish with vegetable oil cooking spray.

In a blender or food processor, combine the brown sugar, flour, oats, cinnamon, nutmeg, and margarine. Blend to a crumbly consistency.

Meanwhile, toss the apple slices and the granulated sugar to coat evenly; place the apples in the baking dish. Scatter the crumb mixture evenly over the apples.

Bake about 35 minutes or until the topping is lightly golden brown and the apples are tender when pierced with a fork. Serve warm or cold.

Variation:
This is also wonderful with fresh peaches.

APPLE CRISP WITH CIDER SAUCE

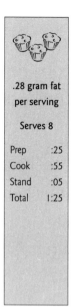

.28 gram fat
per serving

Serves 8

Prep	:25
Cook	:55
Stand	:05
Total	1:25

7 to 8 cups peeled, cored, and sliced apples (each apple will
   equal about 1 cup)
½ cup raisins
¾ cup apple cider
1 cup low-fat graham cracker crumbs (about 12 crackers)
½ cup granulated sugar
½ cup packed brown sugar
1 teaspoon ground cinnamon
¼ teaspoon ground nutmeg
⅓ cup quick-cooking rolled oats
2 tablespoons fat-free margarine, chilled
½ cup pourable fat-free margarine
Apple cider sauce (see page 113)

Preheat the oven to 350 degrees. Arrange apples and
raisins in an 11 x 7-inch baking dish lightly sprayed with
vegetable oil cooking spray. Pour apple cider over the apples and raisins.

In a bowl, mix the crumbs, granulated sugar, brown
sugar, cinnamon, nutmeg, and oats. Cut in both margarines,
mixing to moisten all until crumbly. Sprinkle evenly over
the apple mixture.

Bake until apples are tender, about 50 to 55 minutes.
Serve warm with fat-free ice cream and apple cider sauce.

CHERRY CRISP

Quick–easy–pretty–yum!

1 (21-ounce) can cherry pie filling
1 (16-ounce) can pitted dark sweet cherries, drained
⅔ cup quick-cooking rolled oats
½ cup all-purpose flour
¾ teaspoon ground cinnamon
½ cup packed brown sugar
¼ cup chopped nuts (optional)
¼ cup (4 tablespoons) pourable fat-free margarine

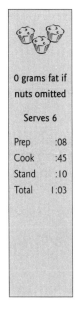

0 grams fat if
nuts omitted

Serves 6

Prep	:08
Cook	:45
Stand	:10
Total	1:03

Preheat the oven to 350 degrees. Have ready an ungreased 8-inch square baking dish.

Combine the pie filling and the sweet cherries in the baking dish and stir to mix.

In a mixing bowl, stir the oats with the flour, cinnamon, brown sugar, and nuts. Pour the margarine over and mix with your hands or a fork until crumbly. Sprinkle over the cherries.

Bake uncovered for 40 to 45 minutes or until lightly browned and bubbly. Serve warm with fat-free ice cream or yogurt.

BERRY GRUNT

**2 grams fat
per serving**

Serves 8

Prep	:25
Cook	:45
Stand	:20
Total	1:30

This is a very old recipe. Grandma used to make it because it would go a long way, and she used any and all berries she could come up with. She would tell me that the name of this pie was berry grunt because it would "grunt" while it was baking. Do you believe her? I wonder, but not enough to get in the oven with the pie.

1 cup sugar, 4 tablespoons reserved
1½ tablespoons cornstarch
¼ cup cold water
3½ cups blueberries
1 cup blackberries
1 cup raspberries
1 tablespoon fresh lemon juice
¼ teaspoon ground cinnamon

BISCUITS:

1¾ cups self-rising flour
1¼ cups fat-free milk

Preheat the oven to 375 degrees. Lightly spray a 2- or 3-quart baking dish with vegetable oil cooking spray. Set aside.

Combine ¾ cup of the sugar, reserving 4 spoonfuls, and the cornstarch in a medium-size saucepan. When blended, stir in ¼ cup of cold water. Place over medium heat and add 1 cup of the blueberries. Bring to a boil, stirring occasionally. Reduce the heat and simmer until thickened. Watch carefully—this will take only a minute or two.

Remove from the heat and stir in the remaining blueberries, the blackberries, raspberries, and lemon juice. Pour into the prepared baking dish.

Mix the reserved sugar and the cinnamon together; set aside.

Put the self-rising flour in a mixing bowl and add the milk; stir just until moistened—the dough will be sticky. Drop large tablespoons of the dough on top of the berries, making about 8 biscuits and leaving space between. Sprinkle the sugar mixture over the biscuits.

Bake uncovered for 40 to 45 minutes or until the fruit is bubbling and the biscuits are nice and brown. Let cool for about 20 minutes before serving. A scoop of fat-free vanilla ice cream is soooo good with hot berry grunt.

Grandma use to cook berry grunt on top of the stove in a great big black cast-iron dutch oven, putting the lid on and letting it simmer on the back of the wood stove while we played on the floor. I can't remember hearing it "grunt" but I guess I wasn't paying enough attention. The reason she cooked it on top of the stove was that the ovens in the woodstoves were so small and she always had to bake bread. Every meal had homemade hot bread — but what else? There was no light bread in a plastic wrapper. And we think we have a tough time of it, going to the supermarket and choosing which one of those breads to take home, reading the label to see how much fat each slice has. . . . It's really a tough job, don't you think? Think again!!

HOT FRUIT COBBLER

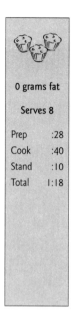

0 grams fat

Serves 8

Prep	:28
Cook	:40
Stand	:10
Total	1:18

1 cup all-purpose flour
1 tablespoon baking powder
2½ cups sugar
1 cup fat-free milk
½ cup pourable fat-free margarine
6 to 8 cups peeled, cored, and sliced fruit, such as peaches, apples
½ teaspoon ground cinnamon
¼ cup water if needed

Preheat the oven to 350 degrees. Lightly spray a 8 x 12 x 2-inch baking pan with vegetable oil cooking spray.

In a mixing bowl, combine the flour, baking powder, and 1 cup of the sugar. Stir until blended. Add the milk and the margarine; mix well and pour into the prepared baking pan.

Place the fruit in a large saucepan and stir in the remaining 1½ cups of sugar and the cinnamon. Stir over medium heat until heated through. If the fruit is not very juicy, add the ¼ cup of water to keep it from scorching.

When nice and hot, pour the fruit evenly over the batter. Bake uncovered for 40 to 45 minutes. Serve warm.

FRUIT COBBLER CAKE

1 (18¼-ounce) package reduced-fat yellow cake mix
¾ cup flavored yogurt (see Note)
¾ cup egg substitute
1 (20-ounce) can fruit pie filling—your choice

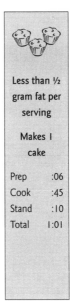

Less than ½
gram fat per
serving

Makes 1
cake

Prep	:06
Cook	:45
Stand	:10
Total	1:01

Preheat the oven to 350 degrees. Lightly coat a 13 x 9 x 2-inch baking dish with vegetable oil cooking spray.

In a medium-size mixing bowl, combine the cake mix with the yogurt and the egg substitute. Start to blend slowly with an electric mixer. When the cake mix is moistened, increase the speed and continue to mix for an additional 2 minutes. Pour the batter into the prepared baking dish, spreading evenly.

With a tablespoon, spoon the pie filling over the batter at random—a dollop here and a dollop there. Now take your spoon and start swirling the filling through the batter, staying on top of the batter as much as possible. It will sink later.

When all the filling is swirled through, place in the oven and bake for 40 to 45 minutes or until a toothpick inserted near the center of the cake (not touching the fruit) comes out clean.

Cool for at least 10 minutes before cutting.

Note: Choose a complementary flavor of yogurt to go with the pie filling (if using peach, choose peach).

NO-BRAINER FRUIT CAKE

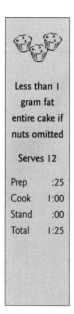

Less than 1
gram fat
entire cake if
nuts omitted

Serves 12

Prep	:25
Cook	1:00
Stand	:00
Total	1:25

1 (21-ounce) can cherry pie filling
1 (19-ounce) can crushed pineapple, juice and all
1 (18¼-ounce) package reduced-fat white cake mix
½ cup fat-free margarine, melted
1 cup applesauce
¼ cup finely chopped nuts (optional)

Preheat the oven to 325 degrees.

Put the cherry pie filling into a 13 x 9 x 2-inch glass baking dish and spread evenly. Pour the pineapple and its juice over the cherries.

Sprinkle the dry cake mix over the fruit.

Melt the margarine in a saucepan. Stir in the applesauce. Pour the mixture evenly over the cake mix and sprinkle with nuts.

Bake uncovered for 50 to 60 minutes or until done to the touch. Serve with a scoop of fat-free vanilla ice cream or frozen yogurt if desired.

LAZY DAZE FRUIT BAKE

½ cup (8 tablespoons) pourable fat-free margarine
1 cup sugar
1 cup all-purpose flour
2 teaspoons baking powder
½ teaspoon salt
¾ cup fat-free milk
1 (21-ounce) can sliced peaches (or use any desired fruit, such as apricots, pineapple, pears, cherries), undrained

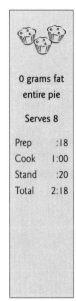

0 grams fat
entire pie

Serves 8

Prep	:18
Cook	1:00
Stand	:20
Total	2:18

Preheat the oven to 350 degrees. Pour the margarine into an 11 x 7 x 1½-inch baking dish and spread it evenly over the bottom.

In a mixing bowl, combine the sugar, flour, baking powder, and salt. Blend with a whisk. Add the milk and stir with a kitchen fork just until the dry ingredients are moistened.

Spoon the dough over the margarine in the baking dish, carefully spreading it to cover the surface evenly.

Chop or cut the peach slices into small, thin pieces. (I cut mine crosswise and arrange evenly in a single layer.) Cover the dough with the fruit and its juices.

Bake uncovered for about 60 minutes or until done to the touch and nicely browned. Let cool in the baking dish on a wire rack for 20 minutes.

QUICK FRUIT BAKE

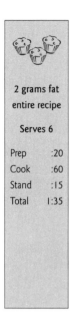

**2 grams fat
entire recipe**

Serves 6

Prep	:20
Cook	:60
Stand	:15
Total	1:35

5 slices day-old bread (to make 1¼ cups bread crumbs)
¼ cup solid-type fat-free margarine
¼ cup packed brown sugar
¼ teaspoon ground nutmeg
Grated rind and juice of ½ lemon
3 to 4 apples or peaches, peeled, cored, and sliced thin

Preheat the oven to 350 degrees. Lightly coat an 11 x 7 x 1½-inch baking dish with vegetable oil cooking spray.

For freshly made bread crumbs: Tear the bread slices into large pieces and place in a blender or a food processor fitted with the metal blade. Pulse 5 or 6 times, until fine crumbs are formed.

Measure 1¼ cups of crumbs and return them to the blender. Add the margarine and pulse to blend. Set aside.

In a mixing bowl, combine the brown sugar, nutmeg, and lemon rind and juice. Toss with the sliced fruit.

Cover the bottom of the prepared baking dish with a layer of crumbs. Place half the fruit evenly over the crumbs. Repeat the bread crumb layer, then a layer of the remaining fruit, and top with a thin layer of crumbs. Lightly spray with butter-flavored cooking spray.

Bake uncovered for about 60 minutes or until the fruit is soft and the crumbs are lightly browned.

APPLE BAKE

Quick and easy to make.

4 to 5 apples
Lemon juice
1 (8-ounce) package fat-free cream cheese, at room temperature
1 cup packed brown sugar
¼ cup plus 2 tablespoons all-purpose flour
¼ cup egg substitute
1 teaspoon ground cinnamon
½ teaspoon vanilla extract
3 tablespoons fat-free margarine

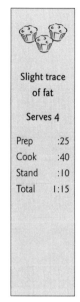

Slight trace
of fat

Serves 4

Prep	:25
Cook	:40
Stand	:10
Total	1:15

Preheat the oven to 350 degrees. Lightly coat an 8-inch square baking dish with vegetable oil cooking spray.

Peel, core, and slice enough apples to measure 4 to 5 cups. Toss with 1 to 2 tablespoons of lemon juice. Set aside.

In a mixing bowl, combine the cream cheese with ½ cup of the brown sugar, 2 tablespoons of the flour, the egg substitute, cinnamon, and vanilla. Stir with a wire whisk until blended (an electric mixer would beat the cream cheese too vigorously and cause it to get thin).

Fold the apples into the cream cheese mixture and transfer to the prepared baking dish.

In a small mixing bowl, combine the remaining ¼ cup of flour and ½ cup of brown sugar. Cut in the margarine with a pastry blender or 2 knives until crumbly. Sprinkle evenly over the apple mixture.

(recipe continues)

Bake uncovered for about 40 minutes or until the apples are soft and the topping is browned. Serve warm or cold.

QUICK FRUIT DESSERT

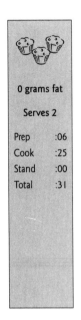

0 grams fat

Serves 2

Prep   :06
Cook   :25
Stand   :00
Total   :31

1 teaspoon lemon juice
1 (16-ounce) can fruit pie filling, your choice
1 cup no-fat granola, without raisins
⅓ cup all-purpose flour
2 tablespoons solid-type fat-free margarine

Preheat the oven to 350 degrees. Spray a 9-inch baking dish lightly with vegetable oil cooking spray.

Mix the lemon juice with the pie filling right in the can—no need to mess up another bowl. Pour into the baking dish.

Combine the granola and flour; mix. Cut in the margarine until crumbly. (I put mine in the blender or food processor. It's quicker and easier.)

Pour the granola over the fruit. Bake for 20 to 25 minutes or until bubbly and golden brown. Serve warm or cold.

Variation:
   Add 2 tablespoons of rolled oats, or ¼ cup chopped nuts to the topping if desired.

EMERGENCY FRUIT PIE

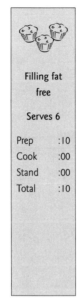

1 (8-ounce) package fat-free cream cheese, at room temperature
1½ cups powdered sugar
1 prepared low-fat graham cracker crust
1 (20-ounce) can fruit pie filling, your choice
1 (12-ounce) package frozen fat-free whipped topping, thawed
¼ cup chopped nuts (optional)

Filling fat free	
Serves 6	
Prep	:10
Cook	:00
Stand	:00
Total	:10

Mix the cream cheese and powdered sugar with a wire whisk until smooth. Pour into the ready pie shell. (You may make your own crust if time permits.)

Fold the fruit pie filling and whipped topping together. Pour over the cream cheese layer. Sprinkle nuts over all.

Place in the freezer until the time needed. Set out about 20 minutes before serving time.

FRUIT TART

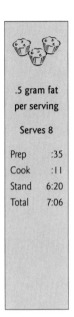

.5 gram fat per serving

Serves 8

Prep	:35
Cook	:11
Stand	6:20
Total	7:06

I am so glad that I (and my friend Marie) got me to learn to like fruit. I just love fresh fruit now.

3 cups low-fat flake-type cereal, such as oat flakes
¼ cup fruit preserves or jam

GLAZE:

½ cup sugar
¼ cup cornstarch
1 (12-ounce) can fruit nectar: peach, apricot, etc. (about 1½ to 1⅔ cups)
4 to 5 cups sliced fresh fruit

Preheat the oven to 375 degrees. Lightly coat a 9- or 10-inch tart pan or pie pan with butter-flavored cooking spray.

In a blender or food processor, crush the cereal flakes to fine crumbs. Add the fruit preserves and continue to process until moist and crumbly. Press the crumbs into the tart pan with your fingers or the back of a spoon (touched with sugar to keep from sticking). Firmly press up the sides; if needed, spray the edges to help hold together and brown slightly.

Bake for 9 to 11 minutes or until the sides feel and look dry. Set aside to cool.

In a medium-size saucepan, combine the sugar and cornstarch, stirring with a wire whisk to blend. Slowly start stirring in the nectar, bringing the heat up to medium; continue to cook and stir until the mixture starts to thicken,

Reduce heat to low and cook, stirring constantly, for about 1 minute longer. Remove from the heat and let the glaze cool for about 20 minutes. (Don't let it get too thick. If it does, simply add a little juice, apple or any kind, to thin.)

While the crust and glaze are cooling, prepare the fruit, peeling and slicing if necessary to thin, attractive slices. Remember eye appeal—you will want to arrange this fruit in nice circles. Slice into thin half moons if using peaches, for example.

Assemble your pie:

Stir the glaze just a little to mix. Spread a thin layer over the crust bottom. Arrange half the fruit in a design as advised above. Spoon a thin layer of glaze over the fruit. Arrange the remaining fruit over, keeping a pretty design going. Spoon the remaining glaze over the fruit. Refrigerate for several hours or until the glaze is set. Cut into wedges and serve. If desired, serve fat-free ice cream or yogurt alongside.

Variation:

> *Use several different types of fresh fruit, such as peaches, blueberries, and strawberries—whatever fruit is in season. Not only is the pie pretty but it's "oh, so good."*

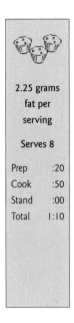

MYSTERY PIE

**2.25 grams
fat per
serving**

Serves 8

Prep	:20
Cook	:50
Stand	:00
Total	1:10

½ cup all-purpose flour

½ cup sugar

1 teaspoon baking powder

Pinch of salt

½ stick (8 tablespoons) reduced-fat margarine, melted

½ cup fat-free milk

1 (16-ounce) can fruit pie filling (cherry, peach, pineapple,
   blueberry, etc.)

Preheat the oven to 350 degrees. Coat a 1½- or 2-quart baking dish with vegetable oil cooking spray.

Blend the flour, sugar, baking powder, and salt in a mixing bowl.

In a separate bowl, combine the melted margarine and the milk. Pour the margarine mixture into the baking dish.

Pour the flour mixture evenly over the margarine mixture. DO NOT STIR.

Pour the pie filling evenly over the flour mixture. DO NOT STIR.

Bake for 45 to 50 minutes. Surprise—you have a pie.

BLUEBERRY CHILL

This pie is called the Turquoise Pie in our house. The first time I made it, I picked up Berry Blue Jell-O at the store instead of Blueberry. It is as Turquoise as it can be. Bob and I had a big laugh with this one. We said, "It is good tasting but it won't pass the eye appeal test." Who can eat turquoise-colored pie?

1 (3-ounce) package blueberry gelatin dessert mix
1 (4-ounce) package fat-free cream cheese (you may need
   to cut an 8-ounce package in half), at room temperature
1 cup fat-free sour cream
1 (12-ounce) container frozen whipped topping, thawed
1 cup powdered sugar
1 prepared crumb crust

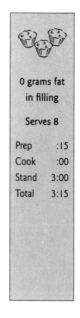

0 grams fat
in filling

Serves 8

Prep   :15
Cook   :00
Stand   3:00
Total   3:15

Mix the gelatin dessert as directed on the package. Place in the refrigerator to chill just until thickened enough so that it mounds on a spoon.

Combine the softened cream cheese, the sour cream, and 1 cup of the whipped topping in a bowl. Fold in powdered sugar. Fold gently to blend. Reserve 1 cup of cream cheese mixture. Spread the remainder over the bottom of the prepared crust.

When the gelatin is thickened but still pourable, reserve about ⅓ of it and pour the rest over the cream cheese layer. (Here you will need to use your guesser. You can guess at about ⅔ of the gelatin.)

Make the topping: Fold the reserved gelatin into the reserved cream cheese mixture. Fold in the remainder of the whipped topping. Return to the refrigerator until time to assemble.

Place the pie in the refrigerator at this time for about 1 hour or until the gelatin is set. When it is set, spread the topping mixture over evenly.

STRAWBERRY PIE

0 grams fat without pastry crust

Serves 6

Prep	:25
Cook	:03
Stand	:40
Total	1:08

1 quart fresh strawberries, rinsed and drained
1 cup sugar
1 level tablespoon cornstarch
1 cup cold water
3 tablespoons strawberry gelatin dessert mix
Red food coloring if desired
1 (9-inch) baked pie crust of your choice, low fat!
Whipped fat-free topping or fat-free ice cream (optional)

Hull and slice the berries. Set aside.

In a medium-size saucepan, combine the sugar and cornstarch. Mix well. Stir in the water and bring to a boil. Cook for 2 or 3 minutes over medium heat until clear.

Remove from the heat. Add the dessert mix; stir to blend and dissolve. If a deeper red color is desired, add red food coloring a few drops at a time.

Add the sliced strawberries; fold to coat evenly. Set aside to cool. When cooled to medium, pour into your prepared baked crust.

Serve with fat-free whipped topping or fat-free frozen yogurt or ice cream.

Variations:

You may substitute blueberries and blueberry gelatin for a blueberry pie, peaches and peach gelatin for peach pie. Just don't forget to change the color of food coloring. It won't look very good with red food coloring in a peach pie. (Just a tease.)

CHERRY DELIGHT

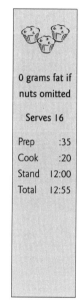

0 grams fat if nuts omitted

Serves 16

Prep	:35
Cook	:20
Stand	12:00
Total	12:55

Any type of pie filling can be used in place of the cherry. Blueberry, apple, peach, strawberry — your choice. Then you will have a different delight.

CRUST:

¾ cup pourable fat-free margarine
1½ cups all-purpose flour
2 tablespoons granulated sugar

TOPPING:

1 (8-ounce) package fat-free cream cheese, at room temperature
2 cups powdered sugar
4 cups frozen fat-free whipped topping, thawed
2 (16-ounce) cans cherry pie filling

Preheat the oven to 350 degrees. Coat a 13 x 9 x 2-inch baking pan with vegetable oil cooking spray.

Make the crust: Combine the margarine, flour, and sugar in a bowl and mix together until crumbly. Spread this mixture evenly over the bottom of the prepared pan. Pat down firmly with your hands. Place in the oven and bake for about 20 minutes. Transfer to a rack and let cool completely.

Make the topping: Put the cream cheese in a large bowl and stir it gently. Mix in the powdered sugar and continue to stir until incorporated. Fold in the whipped topping.

Spread half the topping over the cooled crust. Spread the pie filling over this and top with the remaining cream cheese mixture. Cover with plastic wrap and refrigerate at least 12 hours or overnight.

PEACHY PEACH PIE

Slight trace of fat from spray and oats

Serves 10

Prep	:35
Cook	:40
Stand	:30
Total	1:45

¾ cup sugar
½ teaspoon ground cinnamon
10 to 12 fresh peaches, peeled and sliced

TOPPING:

1½ cups all-purpose flour
1 cup sugar
¼ cup egg substitute
½ cup rolled oats
½ cup fat-free granola without fruit

Preheat the oven to 350 degrees. Lightly coat an 11 x 7 x 1½-inch baking pan with vegetable oil cooking spray.

Combine the ¾ cup of sugar and the cinnamon. Mix well and toss with the sliced peaches to coat them evenly. Pour this mixture into the prepared baking pan.

Make the topping: In a bowl, combine 1 cup of the flour with the cup of sugar and the egg substitute. Mix until crumbly. Pour over the peaches and spread evenly.

In another bowl, combine the remaining ½ cup of flour with the oats and granola. Toss to mix well. Sprinkle evenly over the topping.

Spray the top of the dry layer with butter-flavored cooking spray. Be careful not to blow the oats all over the kitchen—hold the can a distance away and take it easy.

Bake for 35 to 40 minutes or until the crust is nice and brown and the peaches are tender. Let cool on a rack.

PUMPKIN PIE

0 grams fat without crust

Serves 6

Prep	:50
Cook	:50
Stand	:25
Total	2:05

This is also excellent made with cooked and mashed winter squash. We always had tons of squash. Dad didn't know what to do with them and that is when I came up with the squash pie in the early '60s down on the farm.

1¾ cups cooked or canned pumpkin
1¾ cups fat-free milk
1 cup egg substitute
⅔ cup packed brown sugar
2 tablespoons granulated sugar
½ teaspoon ground nutmeg
¼ teaspoon ground cloves
1¼ teaspoons ground cinnamon
½ teaspoon ground ginger
1 teaspoon salt (optional)
1 (9-inch) uncooked pastry shell or crumb crust—low fat!

Preheat the oven to 400 degrees.

In a large bowl, combine the pumpkin, milk, and egg substitute. Mix to blend.

In a separate small container, combine both sugars with the nutmeg, cloves, cinnamon, ginger, and salt. Blend with a wire whisk until thoroughly mixed.

Sprinkle the spice mixture over the pumpkin and beat with an electric mixer at medium speed until blended. Pour into the unbaked shell and bake for 45 to 50 minutes or until a knife inserted near the center comes out clean.

Let cool on a rack.

MAKE-AHEAD PUMPKIN PIE

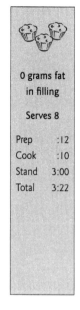

I (9-inch) baked Low-Fat Pie Crust (page 208)
I envelope unflavored gelatin
I teaspoon pumpkin pie spice OR all 4 of the following:
  ½ teaspoon ground nutmeg
  ½ teaspoon ground cinnamon
  ¼ teaspoon ground ginger
  Pinch of salt
I (14-ounce) can fat-free sweetened condensed milk (*not* evaporated milk)
½ cup egg substitute
I (16-ounce) can pumpkin or mashed sweet potatoes (about 2 cups)
Frozen fat-free whipped topping

0 grams fat in filling	
Serves 8	
Prep	:12
Cook	:10
Stand	3:00
Total	3:22

Prepare crust of your choice; let cool.

In a medium-size nonstick saucepan, combine the un-flavored gelatin, your spices (either the pumpkin pie spice or the nutmeg, cinnamon, ginger, and salt). Stir to blend with wire whisk. Add the condensed milk, stirring constantly; add the egg substitute. Let rest for about 45 seconds or one minute. Place over low heat and cook, stirring constantly, until the gelatin dissolves and the mixture thickens slightly—this will take 8 to 10 minutes. Don't lay your whisk down; keep stirring. Remove from the heat and slowly start adding your pumpkin or sweet potatoes. Continue to stir until smooth and well blended. Pour into your pie shell. Chill at least 3 hours, or until set. Garnish with frozen fat-free whipped topping when served.

LEMON CHESS PIE

0 grams fat
without
crust

Serves 6

Prep	:25
Cook	:35
Stand	:30
Total	1:30

2 cups sugar
1 tablespoon flour
1 tablespoon cornmeal
1 cup egg substitute
½ cup applesauce
¼ cup fat-free milk
¼ cup fresh lemon juice
3 to 4 tablespoons grated lemon rind
1 (9-inch) unbaked pie shell, graham cracker or low-fat regular

Preheat the oven to 325 degrees.

Place the sugar, flour, and cornmeal in a large mixing bowl. Blend with a wire whisk or fork.

Add the egg substitute, applesauce, milk, lemon juice, and lemon rind. Mix with an electric mixer until well blended.

Pour into the pie shell. Bake for 35 to 45 minutes or until the top is golden brown. Let cool before serving.

LAYERED LEMON PIE

This is a very lemony pie, both thick and rich. Not too large a serving! You can always offer second helpings. And a small serving keeps guests from feeling guilty for not eating it all.

1 (9-inch) baked pastry shell (pages 209–12), or graham cracker
   crust (page 213)
1 (3-ounce) package cook-and-serve pudding
¼ cup sugar
2 cups plus ¼ cup water
¼ cup egg substitute

TOPPING:

1 (8-ounce) tub fat-free frozen whipped topping, thawed
1 (14-ounce) can fat-free sweetened condensed milk (*not* evaporated milk)
1 (3-ounce) package instant lemon pudding mix less
   1 tablespoonful
Lemon slices and mint leaves for garnish

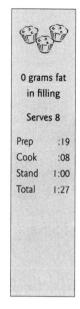

**0 grams fat
in filling**

Serves 8

Prep	:19
Cook	:08
Stand	1:00
Total	1:27

Prepare pastry shell of your choice.

In a medium-size nonstick saucepan, combine the pudding mix, sugar, ¼ cup of the water, and the egg substitute. Mix well with a wire whisk and place over medium heat. Gradually start adding the 2 cups of water, stirring all the time with the whisk. Bring to a full boil, lower the heat to medium low, and continue cooking until thickened. Remove from the heat; let cool for about 5 minutes.

Pour the cooked lemon filling into the pie shell. Allow to cool completely.

Make the topping: In a medium-size bowl, combine the whipped topping and the condensed milk. Stir to mix. Start folding in the instant pudding mix. Don't forget to take out and discard a heaping tablespoonful. Otherwise it will be a little too thick. If it is too thick, add a little more whipped topping.

When completely blended, place the topping in the refrigerator until the filling in your pastry shell is completely cool. If you put it on while it is too hot, it will melt your topping and make a mess.

Assembly: Pour the prepared topping over the filling, spreading to the edges and swirling to make it attractive. Garnish with a lemon slice standing up on top and a couple of mint leaves alongside the lemon. (Cut the lemon and place between thicknesses of paper towel for a short time to keep from being juicy on the pie.)

WHITE CHOCOLATE BANANA PIE

1 cup banana nut crunch cereal
5 medium-size bananas
2 tablespoons lemon juice
2 (3-ounce) packages instant white chocolate pudding mix
2 cups fat-free milk
½ cup sweetened condensed milk (*not* evaporated milk)

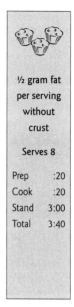

½ gram fat
per serving
without
crust

Serves 8

Prep	:20
Cook	:20
Stand	3:00
Total	3:40

Preheat the oven to 350 degrees. Lightly coat a 9-inch pie plate with vegetable oil cooking spray.

Put the cereal into the container of an electric blender or food processor; blend until the consistency of coarse meal. Peel one of the bananas, cut it into small chunks, and add to the crumbs. Process just until the crumbs are moistened.

Pour the crumbs into the prepared pie plate and pat them to form a crust extending up the sides and evenly over the bottom. Spray lightly with cooking spray. (Warning: don't spray too close to the crust or you will have cereal flying all over the kitchen.) Bake for 15 to 20 minutes or until the edges look dry and lightly browned. Remove from the oven and set aside to cool.

Peel 3 of the remaining bananas and slice them thin. Drizzle with the lemon juice.

Put the pudding mixes in a bowl and add the fat-free milk. Stir with a wire whisk until the mixture starts to thicken. Add the condensed milk and continue stirring until well blended. Gently fold in the sliced bananas with a rubber spatula, trying not to smash them.

Pour the filling into the cooled crust and smooth the top. Refrigerate for about 3 hours to set up nicely. Before serving, slice the remaining banana and arrange in a circle on top of the pie.

If desired, dollop with fat-free whipped topping or sprinkle a bit of dark cocoa powder over the top for garnish.

CUSTARD PIE

0 grams fat
without
crust

Serves 6

Prep	:25
Cook	:45
Stand	:25
Total	1:35

¾ cup egg substitute
2 cups fat-free milk
½ cup sugar
1 dash ground nutmeg
Pinch of salt (optional)
Unbaked 9-inch pie shell

Preheat the oven to 400 degrees.

In a mixing bowl, lightly beat the egg substitute with the milk. Stir in the sugar and a dash of nutmeg along with a small pinch of salt.

Pour into the unbaked pie shell. Bake for 10 minutes; reduce the heat to 300 degrees and continue baking for an additional 35 minutes or until a toothpick or sharp knife inserted in the center comes out clean. Let cool on a rack.

Variation: Egg Custard

> *Divide the custard among 6 individual custard cups and sprinkle with nutmeg. Set the cups in a dry roasting pan; pour hot water into the pan to a depth of 1 inch. Bake uncovered at 325 degrees for about 1 hour. Chill slightly before serving.*

MOCK PECAN PIE

Well, it's not what Momma taught me to make, but it'll do. She was known as the Pecan Pie Queen and passed the secret on to me. I became the PPQ. I have now passed the title on to my daughter and I believe she is prepping her daughter to be the next reigning PPQ. Everyone in the family had their specialty and were expected to bring them to each family gathering. If you didn't show up with your special, you might as well not show up.

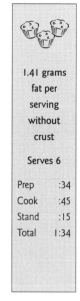

1.41 grams
fat per
serving
without
crust

Serves 6

Prep	:34
Cook	:45
Stand	:15
Total	1:34

1 (9½-inch) unbaked low-fat pie crust (page 208)
⅓ cup fat-free margarine
1 tablespoon lower-fat margarine
⅔ cup sugar
1 cup lite waffle syrup
¾ cup egg substitute
Pinch of salt
½ teaspoon vanilla extract
½ cup nutlike cereal, such as Grape-Nuts
½ cup quick-cooking rolled oats

Preheat the oven to 375 degrees. Have ready a pastry shell of your choice.

In a small saucepan, combine the margarines and place over medium-low heat until heated through, just hot enough to melt the low-fat margarine. Remove from the heat.

Combine the margarine with the sugar and syrup; beat with an electric mixer until blended. Beat in the egg substitute, salt, and vanilla. Sprinkle both the cereals on top and fold them into the egg mixture with a rubber spatula.

Pour into the prepared pastry shell and bake for 40 to 45 minutes or until a knife comes out clean when inserted in the center of the filling. Let cool on a rack.

OATMEAL PIE ("SUBSTITUTE PECAN PIE")

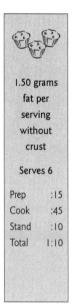

1.50 grams
fat per
serving
without
crust

Serves 6

Prep	:15
Cook	:45
Stand	:10
Total	1:10

½ cup egg substitute

I cup packed brown sugar

¾ cup granulated sugar

I teaspoon vanilla extract

I tablespoon lower-fat margarine, at room temperature

I tablespoon fat-free margarine, at room temperature

I tablespoon shredded coconut, chopped very fine

¾ cup quick-cooking rolled oats

I unbaked low-fat pie shell (page 208)

Preheat the oven to 350 degrees.

In the bowl of an electric mixer, beat the egg substitute at medium speed for about 1 minute. Add the brown sugar; beat until blended. Beat in the granulated sugar, vanilla, and both margarines. When the mixture is well blended, change from a mixer to a rubber spatula and fold in the coconut and the oats.

Pour into the pie shell and bake for 40 to 45 minutes or until a knife inserted in the center of the pie comes out clean. Let cool before cutting.

PISTACHIO PIE

This recipe is very old, but it is still refreshing and pretty, not to mention good tasting.

1 (20-ounce) can crushed pineapple, juice and all
1 (4-ounce) package pistachio instant pudding mix
1 cup miniature marshmallows
¼ cup finely chopped pistachio nuts
2 cups frozen fat-free whipped topping, thawed
1 prebaked graham cracker crust (page 213)

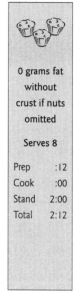

0 grams fat
without
crust if nuts
omitted

Serves 8

Prep	:12
Cook	:00
Stand	2:00
Total	2:12

Put the pineapple and its juice in a mixing bowl. Add the pudding mix and stir until it starts to thicken. Add the marshmallows and pistachios; continue to stir until blended. Stir in the whipped topping.

Pour into the pie shell and spread with the whipped topping. Refrigerate for at least 2 hours before serving.

PISTACHIO PIE WITH CREAM CHEESE

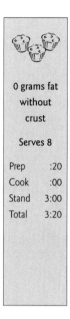

0 grams fat without crust

Serves 8

Prep	:20
Cook	:00
Stand	3:00
Total	3:20

This is nice for Christmas time or Saint Patrick's Day. If serving at Christmas, sprinkle with chopped maraschino cherries for color. On Saint Patrick's Day use green cherries.

BOTTOM LAYER:

1 (8 ounce) package fat-free cream cheese, at room temperature
½ cup powdered sugar
½ teaspoon vanilla extract

1 (9-inch) baked low-fat pie crust (page 208) or purchased low-fat or no-fat crust

FILLING:

1 (12-ounce) container fat-free frozen whipped topping, thawed, divided
½ cup powdered sugar
1 cup fat-free milk
1 (4-ounce) package pistachio instant pudding mix
¾ cup nonfat sweetened condensed milk (*not* evaporated milk)

Combine the bottom-layer ingredients: cream cheese, ½ cup powdered sugar, and ½ teaspoon vanilla. Cream gently with wire whisk. Line pie crust with cream cheese mixture.

Make the filling: Combine 1½ cups of the whipped topping and ½ cup powdered sugar. Blend with a whisk. Set aside.

Pour the fat-free milk into a mixing bowl. Stir in the pudding mix, whisking just until it starts to thicken slightly. Stir in the condensed milk. When well blended, fold in the reserved whipped topping mixture. Blend well.

Pour over the cream cheese mixture in the pie shell. Reserve the remaining whipped topping for garnish; refrigerate until needed.

Refrigerate the pie for 2 or 3 hours or until set. Dollop or spread the remaining whipped topping over the pistachio pudding mixture. If desired, sprinkle a tiny pinch of cocoa over for garnish.

STRAWBERRY PIE WITH MERINGUE CRUST

Strawberries are a suggestion only — you may use your own ideas to fill any crust.

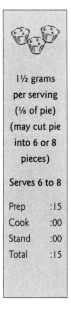

1½ grams
per serving
(⅛ of pie)
(may cut pie
into 6 or 8
pieces)

Serves 6 to 8

Prep	:15
Cook	:00
Stand	:00
Total	:15

4 to 5 cups strawberries
¼ cup sugar
1 Meringue Crust (page 204)
2 squares German sweet chocolate
1 tablespoon reduced-fat margarine
2 cups fat-free frozen whipped topping, thawed

Rinse, drain, and hull the berries. Cut the berries in half and toss with the sugar. Put in a colander and allow to drain until just before serving time.

Melt the chocolate and margarine together in the top of a double boiler. Drizzle over the meringue crust.

Just before serving, top the crust with the drained fruit. Spread with the whipped topping.

(recipe continues)

Variations:

If I am using peaches, I also place them in a colander to drain until time to place in the crust.

You may leave off the chocolate if desired; you will save some grams, but it dresses up your pie.

It is pretty for the summer to use blueberries and strawberries for the Fourth of July, with the whipped topping: red—white—blue.

This is also great for the Christmas holidays. Put a couple of drops of red food coloring in the meringue to make a red or pink crust, or green, and fill with red berries.

MERINGUE CRUST

0 grams fat if
pecans
omitted

Serves 6

Prep   :40
Cook   :45
Stand   12:00
Total   13:25

Make this at least a day ahead, because it has to dry out overnight. (Wrap it airtight for longer storage — it keeps well.)

14 fat-free saltines, to make ½ cup finely crushed
4 egg whites, at room temperature
¼ teaspoon cream of tartar
⅛ teaspoon salt
½ cup sugar
1 teaspoon vanilla extract
¼ cup finely chopped pecans (optional)

Preheat the oven to 300 degrees. Spray a 9-inch pie plate with vegetable oil cooking spray to cover completely.

Put the crackers in a blender or food processor to make fine crumbs. Or you may put the crackers in a plastic zipper bag and crush with a rolling pin to make your crumbs.

In a glass mixing bowl, very clean, beat the egg whites until foamy. Mix in the cream of tartar and salt, and beat until soft peaks form. Gradually start adding sugar, a small portion at a time; continue beating at high speed until stiff peaks form.

Fold the vanilla into the meringue, along with the nuts and the cracker crumbs—just until folded in, not too frisky with your whites.

Spread the meringue mixture into the prepared pie plate and up the sides, smoothing to make the shape of the pie plate.

Bake for 45 minutes. WITHOUT opening the oven door, turn the oven off and leave the meringue in the oven for 10 to 12 hours, or until the next day.

Note: This will show if you are a trusting person or a nosy person. If you can let it dry out without looking, you're a trusting person, and if you can let it dry out without peeking you're not nosy. Can't wait until morning, can you? Have fun in the kitchen.

PINEAPPLE ANGEL PIE

1.40 grams fat

Serves 6

Prep	:45
Cook	:25
Stand	3:30
Total	4:40

Garnish hint: I like to dust the top with cocoa or cinnamon, very lightly.

CRUST:

3 large egg whites
½ teaspoon vanilla extract
½ teaspoon salt
1 cup granulated sugar
21 lower-in-fat Ritz crackers, crushed

FILLING:

1 (8-ounce) package fat-free cream cheese, at room temperature
3 tablespoons fat-free milk
¾ cup powdered sugar

TOP LAYER:

1 (8-ounce) can crushed pineapple, drained
¼ cup finely chopped pecans (optional)
1 (6-ounce) carton frozen whipped topping, thawed

Make the crust: Preheat the oven to 350 degrees. Beat the egg whites in a bowl until foamy. Mix in the vanilla and salt. Gradually add the sugar, a small amount at a time, and continue beating until the whites are glossy and form stiff peaks. With a rubber spatula, fold in the cracker crumbs. Spoon the mixture into a lightly greased 9-inch pie plate and spread with the back of a spoon to cover the bottom and extend about 1 inch higher than the rim of the plate. Make the sides a little thicker than the bottom. Bake for 25 minutes. Remove from the oven and cool completely—this will take about 30 minutes.

Meanwhile, prepare the filling. In a mixing bowl, gently stir the cream cheese with a wire whisk. Add the milk and powdered sugar and stir until blended.

When the crust is completely cooled, line it with the filling. Chill for 3 hours.

Top the pie with the drained pineapple in an even layer. Sprinkle with pecans and spread with the whipped topping.

BASIC PIE CRUST

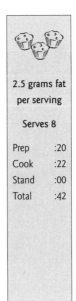

2.5 grams fat
per serving

Serves 8

Prep	:20
Cook	:22
Stand	:00
Total	:42

1¼ cups all-purpose flour
1 tablespoon sugar
¼ teaspoon salt
3 tablespoons chilled solid-type low-fat margarine
4 to 5 tablespoons ice-cold water

Combine the flour, sugar, and salt in a shallow mixing bowl. With a pastry blender or 2 knives, cut in the margarine until crumbly. Start adding ice water, sprinkling over the mixture about 1 tablespoon at a time. Stir lightly with a fork just until a dough ball forms. You may need to add a little more or less water.

Roll out on a floured surface into a circle about 3 inches larger than your pie plate. Transfer to the plate and gently press the bottom and sides.

Trim the pastry so that it hangs evenly about 1 inch over the rim. Roll the overhang under itself so that it is even with the rim; flute the edges.

(recipe continues)

For a prebaked crust: Preheat the oven to 425 degrees. Prick the bottom and sides of the pastry with a fork. To minimize shrinking, lay a sheet of foil over the pastry and fill with dried beans or pie weights. Bake for 10 to 12 minutes; remove the weights and foil and bake another 10 minutes.

LOW-FAT PIE CRUST

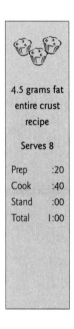

4.5 grams fat
entire crust
recipe

Serves 8

Prep	:20
Cook	:40
Stand	:00
Total	1:00

I cup all-purpose flour
I teaspoon sugar
I tablespoon fat-free margarine
I tablespoon low-fat margarine
¼ cup egg substitute

Combine the flour and sugar in a bowl. Cut in the margarines with a pastry blender or 2 knives until crumbly. Add the egg substitute; mix lightly with a fork until the dough forms a ball.

Roll out on a floured surface or pat into a pie plate. You will need to flour your fingers to keep dough from sticking to them. Bake 30 to 40 minutes.

You may also use this for cobbler. Roll out and cut half the dough into strips for the top. If making an old-fashioned cobbler, with crust on the bottom and up the sides as well as crust in strips on the top, double the recipe.

PIE CRUST I

(My ex-mother-in-law was a very old-fashioned lady, born and raised in the country as am I, but she had no pastry blender. She could take her ingredients and blend them perfectly with her fingers. She would just start pinching the solid fat being used with the flour; pretty soon it was just perfect. She used to try and teach me to do that, and she sure got a lot of laughs. Mine would come out looking like I had been making clay marbles or something. I always got too big of a pinch. A blender is so much easier, at least for me.)

Pinch of salt
2 tablespoons sugar
1½ cups all-purpose flour
3 tablespoons solid-type reduced-fat margarine, chilled
5 to 6 tablespoons ice-cold fat-free milk

½ gram fat per serving

Serves 8

Prep	:20
Cook	:25
Stand	:00
Total	:45

Blend the salt and sugar with the flour until evenly mixed. Add the cold margarine and blend with a pastry bender until the margarine resembles pea-sized crumbles. If no pastry blender is available, use 2 knives or a fork.

When the coarse crumbly stage is reached, use a fork to lightly sprinkle the milk over the flour, 1 tablespoonful at a time. When the dough forms a ball, turn it out onto a floured pastry cloth or surface.

With a rolling pin, start rolling from the center, rotating the dough, until it forms a circle about 2 inches larger than your pie pan. Pick up the crust by rolling it onto the rolling pin, unwrap over the pie plate, pushing it gently down into the pan and arranging carefully with your fingers. Flute or crimp the edges your favorite way.

Prebake the crust if desired (see page 208) or follow your pie recipe.

PIE CRUST II

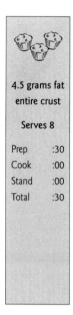

**4.5 grams fat
entire crust**

Serves 8

Prep	:30
Cook	:00
Stand	:00
Total	:30

1¼ cups all-purpose flour
Pinch of salt
1 tablespoon solid-type fat-free margarine
1 tablespoon solid-type light margarine
¼ cup cold fat-free milk

Combine the flour and salt in a mixing bowl; stir to blend. Add both margarines, using a pastry blender or fork; mix until crumbly.

Start adding the milk 1 tablespoon at a time, tossing with a fork until the dough holds together. This may require more or less milk.

Form the dough into a ball. Roll out on a floured surface and place over a pie plate. Pat the dough against the bottom all around. Cut off any excess hanging over and shape the edges with fingers or a fork.

Prebake the crust if desired (see page 208) or follow your pie recipe.

PIE CRUST III

1¼ cups nutlike cereal, such as Grape-Nuts
¼ cup finely chopped nuts
2 tablespoons packed brown sugar
3 tablespoons egg substitute

Preheat the oven to 350 degrees.

Mix the cereal, nuts, and brown sugar in a bowl. Stir in the egg substitute, mixing until crumbly. Turn into a 9-inch pie plate, pressing up the sides and smoothing out nicely over the bottom.

Bake for 12 to 14 minutes. Let cool and fill. If using a hot filling, no cooling time is required.

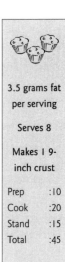

2.25 grams
fat if nuts
omitted
(entire crust)

Makes 1 9-
inch crust

Prep	:06
Cook	:14
Stand	:45
Total	1:05

COCONUT CRUST

1 cup quick cooking rolled oats
⅓ cup all-purpose flour
3 tablespoons packed brown sugar
2 tablespoons lower-in-fat grated coconut
3 tablespoons light margarine, melted
½ teaspoon coconut-flavored extract

Spray a 9-inch pie pan with vegetable oil cooking spray; set aside. Preheat the oven to 350 degrees.

In a large mixing bowl, combine the oats, flour, brown sugar, and coconut. Toss to mix well. Add the margarine and flavoring. Stir until the mixture is moist and crumbly.

3.5 grams fat
per serving

Serves 8

Makes 1 9-
inch crust

Prep	:10
Cook	:20
Stand	:15
Total	:45

Press the crust over the bottom and up the sides of the pie pan, using your fingers or the back of a spoon. You may want to dip your fingers or the spoon into sugar to keep crumbs from sticking.

Bake for 20 minutes. Let cool to room temperature. Fill as desired.

SPICED CRUMB CRUST

2 grams fat
per serving

Serves 12

Prep	:22
Cook	:10
Stand	:00
Total	:32

This is a great crust recipe for just about anything you would like to top it with: cheesecake, fruit bars, and many other suggestions throughout the book.

1¼ cups freshly made bread crumbs
¾ cup nutlike cereal
½ cup granulated sugar
¼ teaspoon ground cinnamon
¼ teaspoon ground nutmeg
¼ cup applesauce
2 tablespoons light margarine, melted
1 egg white

Preheat the oven to 350 degrees.

Make bread crumbs with day-old bread in the food processor or blender. Combine the crumbs, cereal, sugar, cinnamon, and nutmeg in a medium-size mixing bowl. Blend together.

Add the applesauce, margarine, and egg white; mix with a fork until just moistened. Press into the bottom of a 9-

inch springform pan lightly sprayed with vegetable oil cooking spray.

Bake 10 minutes and set aside.

GRAHAM CRACKER CRUMB PIE CRUST

6 tablespoons low-fat margarine
1½ cups low-fat graham cracker crumbs (10 to 12 double graham
   crackers; crush in blender or food processor or crush in plastic
   bag with rolling pin)
3 tablespoons sugar

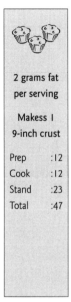

2 grams fat
per serving

Makess 1
9-inch crust

Prep	:12
Cook	:12
Stand	:23
Total	:47

Preheat the oven to 350 degrees.

Melt the margarine in a small saucepan. Remove from the heat and let cool 3 minutes.

Place the crushed crumbs in a medium bowl, add sugar, and mix until evenly blended.

Drizzle the melted margarine over the crumbs. Mix with fork or fingers until moistened and thoroughly combined.

Press evenly into the bottom and sides of a 9-inch pie pan. Bake for 10 to 12 minutes, or until crust just begins to brown. Don't overbake. Let cool to room temperature before filling.

Puddings, Jellies, Trifles, and Layered and Frozen Desserts

BREAD PUDDING

This is a recipe (made lighter) that my great-aunt taught me when I was nine years old.

6 to 8 slices day-old bread, torn into small pieces
½ cup water
2 tablespoons all-purpose flour
¼ teaspoon salt
¾ cup sugar
¾ cup egg substitute
2 teaspoons vanilla extract
3 cups fat-free milk

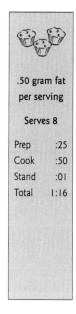

.50 gram fat
per serving

Serves 8

Prep	:25
Cook	:50
Stand	:01
Total	1:16

Preheat the oven to 375 degrees. Lightly spray a 2-quart casserole with vegetable oil cooking spray.

Place the torn pieces of bread in the casserole. Sprinkle with water, trying to moisten all, then stir and crumble the bread to moisten and break up the pieces. (I just use my hands; they were here a long time before the utensils. Besides, a good cook cooks with her hands.) Smash and squeeze into a pulplike consistency. Let stand about 1 minute.

In a bowl, mix the flour and salt into the sugar, then pour over the bread. Stir to mix. Mix the egg substitute, vanilla, and milk. Stir into the bread until well blended.

Bake uncovered for 50 to 60 minutes or until nicely browned and puffed up. The pudding will lose some of the puffy air as it cools, so don't panic.

RAISIN BREAD PUDDING WITH WARM SAUCE

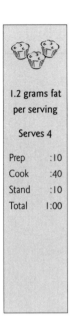

1.2 grams fat per serving

Serves 4

Prep	:10
Cook	:40
Stand	:10
Total	1:00

4 to 5 slices bread, toasted and cubed

3 tablespoons raisins

1½ cups fat-free milk

½ cup egg substitute

¼ cup sugar, plus 1 teaspoon reserved for sauce

1 teaspoon vanilla extract

2 tablespoons all-purpose flour

½ cup apple juice or cider

Preheat the oven to 350 degrees. Lightly coat a 1-quart casserole with vegetable oil cooking spray.

Place the bread cubes and raisins in the casserole. In a small mixing bowl, combine the milk, egg substitute, ¼ cup sugar, and vanilla. Mix with a wire whisk. Pour the milk mixture over the bread and stir until evenly coated.

Bake uncovered for about 35 minutes or until a knife inserted in the center comes out clean. Let cool slightly on a wire rack before serving.

Sauce: Stir the 1 teaspoon reserved sugar and the flour together in a small pan, add cider and stir until well blended. Cook over medium heat until the sauce starts to thicken, stirring constantly. Drizzle over the pudding, dividing evenly over 4 servings. A scoop of fat-free ice cream or frozen yogurt is not bad on the side.

HARVEST-TIME BREAD PUDDING

10 slices day-old bread, cut into ¼-inch cubes
⅛ teaspoon ground cloves
¾ teaspoon ground cinnamon
½ teaspoon ground nutmeg
1 cup packed brown sugar
½ cup granulated sugar
1 tablespoon all-purpose flour
1 cup egg substitute
2 cups fat-free milk
1 cup mashed pumpkin
1 teaspoon vanilla extract

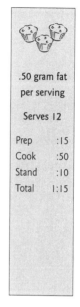

.50 gram fat
per serving

Serves 12

Prep	:15
Cook	:50
Stand	:10
Total	1:15

Preheat the oven to 350 degrees. Lightly coat a 13 x 9 x 2-inch baking dish with vegetable oil cooking spray.

In a large mixing bowl, combine bread cubes, cloves, cinnamon, and nutmeg. Toss to mix well.

In a medium-size mixing bowl, combine the brown sugar, granulated sugar, and flour. Add the egg substitute, milk, and pumpkin. Blend well. Add vanilla and continue to mix with a wire whisk. When nice and smooth, pour over bread crumbs and gently stir to cover all. Let stand about 10 minutes.

Pour into the prepared baking dish and bake for 40 to 50 minutes, or until a knife inserted into the center comes out clean.

This is very good served with a nice warm vanilla sauce.

Variation:

> Use mashed cooked winter squash or sweet potatoes instead of pumpkin.

LEMON BREAD PUDDING WITH LEMON SAUCE

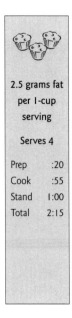

**2.5 grams fat
per 1-cup
serving**

Serves 4

Prep   :20
Cook   :55
Stand   1:00
Total   2:15

1¾ cups buttermilk (fat-free, if possible, or 1 gram per cup)
¾ cup sugar
¾ cup egg substitute
⅓ cup fresh lemon juice
2 tablespoons pourable fat-free margarine
2 teaspoons grated lemon rind
8 slices French bread, ½ inch thick, cut into 1-inch squares

LEMON SAUCE:

½ cup sugar
2 tablespoons cornstarch
1¼ cups cold water
¼ cup fresh lemon juice
½ teaspoon grated lemon rind

Lightly spray a 2-quart casserole or an 11 x 7-inch baking dish with vegetable oil cooking spray. Set aside.

Combine the buttermilk, sugar, egg substitute, lemon juice, margarine, and grated lemon rind in a large mixing bowl. Add the bread cubes and toss to mix well. Let stand about 1 hour.

Preheat the oven to 350 degrees.

Spoon the bread mixture into the prepared baking dish and bake uncovered for 50 to 55 minutes or until the pudding is set. Serve warm or at room temperature with lemon sauce.

To make the lemon sauce: In a small heavy saucepan, combine the sugar and cornstarch. Blend with a whisk and gradually add the water and lemon juice. Set over medium heat. Stirring constantly, bring to a boil and cook about 2 or 3 minutes. Remove from the heat, let cool, and stir in the lemon rind. Serve over pudding or any dessert. The sauce may be stored up to a week in the refrigerator.

PINEAPPLE PUDDING

2 cups granulated sugar
½ cup fat-free margarine, at room temperature
½ cup applesauce
¾ cup egg substitute
1 (14-ounce) can crushed pineapple, juice and all
4 cups very dry bread crumbs or pieces cut into 1-inch squares
   (see Note)
¼ cup fat-free milk

4 grams fat
entire
pudding

Serves 12

Prep	:25
Cook	1:00
Stand	:00
Total	1:25

Preheat the oven to 350 degrees. Prepare a 13 x 9 x 2-inch baking dish: spray lightly with butter-flavored cooking spray.

Cream together the sugar, margarine, and applesauce in a large mixing bowl. Stir in the egg substitute, well beaten.

Fold in the pineapple, then fold in the dry bread. Stir in the milk. Spoon into the prepared baking dish. Bake uncovered for 1 hour.

(recipe continues)

Note: I toast my old bread and let cool and dry during the time I am putting together the pudding. Can be done the day ahead.

CHOCOLATE RICE PUDDING

2 grams
fat entire
pudding

Serves 8

Prep	:10
Cook	1:20
Stand	2:00
Total	3:30

¼ cup unsweetened cocoa powder
½ cup sugar
½ teaspoon ground cinnamon
¼ teaspoon salt
¾ cup egg substitute
2 cups fat-free milk
I teaspoon vanilla extract
I ½ cups cooked rice

Preheat the oven to 375 degrees. Spray a 2-quart baking dish with cooking oil spray, butter flavored if available.

Combine in a small bowl the cocoa, sugar, cinnamon, and salt. In a large mixing bowl, mix the egg substitute with the sugar mixture. Use a wire whisk to blend. When blended, add the milk, about ½ cup at a time, stirring to blend well. Stir in the vanilla. Fold in the rice. Pour into the prepared baking dish.

Place a large baking pan or roasting pan on the middle rack of your oven. Set the pudding dish in the center of the larger pan. Pour enough hot water into the larger pan to come about ⅔ up the dish of pudding.

Bake uncovered for 1 hour, stirring after 20 minutes, then stirring again after baking about 40 minutes. Continue to bake another 20 minutes or until a knife inserted in the middle of the pudding comes out clean.

Cool completely before serving.

PISTACHIO PARFAIT

1 (21-ounce) can crushed pineapple, juice and all
1 (4-ounce) package pistachio instant pudding mix
1 (12-ounce) package fat-free frozen whipped topping, thawed
1 cup miniature marshmallows
¼ cup finely chopped nuts (optional)

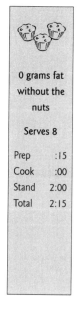

0 grams fat
without the
nuts

Serves 8

Prep	:15
Cook	:00
Stand	2:00
Total	2:15

Combine the pineapple and its juice in a bowl with the pudding mix. Stir to blend. Fold in the whipped topping, marshmallows, and nuts if using. Refrigerate for 1 to 2 hours before serving.

FROSTED FRUIT GEL

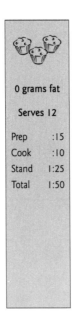

0 grams fat

Serves 12

Prep	:15
Cook	:10
Stand	1:25
Total	1:50

2 (0.3-ounce) packages sugar-free lemon gelatin dessert mix
1 (21-ounce) can crushed pineapple, juice reserved
3 medium bananas, peeled and sliced
1½ cups miniature marshmallows

FROSTING:

⅔ cup sugar
1 tablespoon all-purpose flour
¼ cup egg substitute
1 (12-ounce) carton fat-free frozen whipped topping, thawed

Dissolve the dessert mix in a bowl according to package instructions. Let thicken slightly in the refrigerator, about 1 hour.

Add the drained pineapple (juice reserved), bananas, and marshmallows. Pour into a shallow rectangular dish, about 13 x 9 or 11 x 8 inches. Return to the refrigerator until ready to frost.

To prepare frosting: Combine the sugar, flour, egg substitute, and reserved pineapple juice in the top pan of a double boiler. Bring water to a boil in the lower pan, stirring the sugar mixture. Continue to stir and cook over gently boiling water until thick.

Let cool completely, spread over the chilled fruit, then spread with the whipped topping.

LAYERED CHERRY DESSERT

1 (3-ounce) package lemon-flavored gelatin dessert mix
1½ cups boiling water
½ (8-ounce) package fat-free cream cheese, at room temperature
1 teaspoon grated lemon rind
1 envelope unflavored gelatin
2 tablespoons lemon juice
¼ teaspoon ground cinnamon
1 (21-ounce) can cherry pie filling

0 grams fat	
Serves 8	
Prep	:35
Cook	:00
Stand	3:00
Total	3:35

In a 2- or 3-quart bowl, dissolve the lemon-flavored gelatin in 1 cup of the boiling water. Stir until the gelatin is completely dissolved. With a wire whisk, stir in the cream cheese and lemon rind until smooth. Pour into a 5-cup mold; refrigerate until firm, about 1½ hours.

In a separate bowl soften the unflavored gelatin in lemon juice. Stir in the remaining ½ cup of boiling water until the gelatin is all dissolved. Stir in the cinnamon and cherry pie filling. Pour over the cream cheese mixture. Refrigerate until firm. Unmold. Garnish with fat-free whipped topping if desired and long-stemmed maraschino cherries.

CRANBERRY HOLIDAY DELIGHT

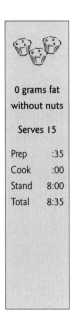

0 grams fat
without nuts

Serves 15

Prep   :35
Cook   :00
Stand   8:00
Total   8:35

2 unpeeled oranges

3 cups fresh or frozen cranberries

2 (0.3-ounce) package sugar-free lemon gelatin dessert mix

2 cups hot water

2 apples, cored and sliced, unpeeled

1¾ cups sugar

¼ teaspoon salt

¼ cup finely chopped pecans (optional)

1½ cups fat-free mayonnaise

3 cups whipped fat-free frozen topping, thawed

Have ready a 13 x 9 x 2-inch glass baking dish.

Cut the oranges into 1-inch cubes and remove the seeds. Place in a blender or food processor and pulse until coarsely chopped. Remove to the baking dish.

Rinse and drain the cranberries. Chop coarsely in the blender or food processor and add to the oranges.

Dissolve the gelatin in hot water. Add to the oranges and cranberries. Stir in the sliced apples, sugar, salt, and pecans if using. Mix well. Place in the refrigerator for 3 or 4 hours, or until firm.

Prepare the topping: Blend together the mayonnaise and whipped topping. Spread over the cranberry dessert.

SAVORY CHRISTMAS TREAT

¾ cup red hots (candy)
1 cup boiling water
1 (4-ounce) package red gelatin dessert mix, any flavor
1½ cups applesauce
½ cup fat-free mayonnaise
1 (8-ounce) package fat-free cream cheese, at room temperature
¼ cup finely chopped nuts (optional)
½ cup finely chopped celery

0 grams fat
without nuts

Serves 8

Prep	:15
Cook	:00
Stand	3:00
Total	3:15

Add the red hots to the cup of boiling water in a saucepan and stir until dissolved.

Add the gelatin mix and applesauce. Stir to blend. Pour half this mixture into a shallow glass dish measuring about 11 x 7 inches. Refrigerate until set.

Leave the reserved half at room temperature.

Combine the mayonnaise, cream cheese, nuts, and celery and pour over the set gelatin mixture. This mixture will be stiff, so spread very gently.

Pour the reserved half of the gelatin mixture over the cream cheese mixture. Return to the refrigerator for at least 2 hours or until set.

TRIPLE-LAYER FRUIT DESSERT

1.5 grams
per serving

Serves 12

Prep	:32
Cook	:20
Stand	2:50
Total	3:42

CRUST:

2 cups all-purpose flour

2 tablespoons granulated sugar

½ cup solid-type fat-free margarine

½ stick (4 tablespoons) reduced-fat margarine

1 (6-ounce) package berry gelatin dessert mix of your choice

2 cups boiling water

2 (10-ounce) packages frozen berries, thawed

1 (8-ounce) package fat-free cream cheese, at room temperature

1 cup powdered sugar

1 teaspoon vanilla extract

2 cups fat-free frozen whipped topping, thawed, plus additional
topping for garnish

Preheat the oven to 350 degrees.

In a mixing bowl, stir together the flour and sugar. Add both margarines and cut in with a pastry blender or 2 knives until the mixture resembles coarse crumbs. Press into the bottom of a 13 x 9 x 2-inch baking pan to form a crust. Bake for 20 to 25 minutes or until firm. The crust will not brown, so be careful not to overbake. Remove from the oven and let cool in the pan on a rack.

In a bowl, dissolve the gelatin mix in the boiling water and stir in the berries. Chill until the mixture begins to thicken, at least 20 minutes. (This will be the third layer.)

In a separate bowl, stir the cream cheese gently with a wire whisk. Stir in the powdered sugar and vanilla and mix until well combined. Fold in the whipped topping.

When the crust has cooled completely, spread with the cream cheese mixture. Spoon the gelatin over the cheese layer. Refrigerate until set. To serve, cut into squares and garnish with whipped topping.

STRAWBERRY CHOCOLATE CREAM

1 recipe graham cracker crust (page 213)

2 plus 1⅔ cups fat-free milk

2 (3-ounce) packages instant fat-free white chocolate pudding mix

1 (14-ounce) can nonfat sweetened condensed milk (*not* evaporated milk)

Reserved bag of crumbs from cheesecake mix

3 cups sliced fresh strawberries (reserve 1 large berry for garnish)

1 (13.6-ounce) package no-bake strawberry cheesecake mix (reduced fat)

1.5 grams fat per serving	
Serves 15	
Prep	:50
Cook	:00
Stand	2:00
Total	2:50

A 13 x 9 x 2-inch clear baking dish is best for this; it lets your pretty dessert show through.

Prepare the pie crust according to recipe directions. Press it onto the bottom of the baking dish and just a tiny bit up the sides. Bake according to recipe instructions.

In a bowl, combine 2 cups of fat-free milk with the 2 boxes of instant pudding mix; blend with a wire whisk until the mixture begins to thicken. Pour in the condensed milk and continue to mix until smooth. Pour into pie crust. Smooth out evenly.

Sprinkle the bagful of graham cracker crumbs over the pudding layer. Place the sliced, drained strawberries in a layer over the crumbs.

In the same mixing bowl used for the pudding mix, combine the bag of cheesecake mix and remaining 1⅔ cups fat-free milk; blend until smooth and thickened. Pour over the layer of strawberries.

Drizzle the bag of strawberry glaze from the cheesecake mix over all. You may also desire to drizzle chocolate (fat-free) ice cream topping over. Slice the reserved large strawberry into thin slices connected at the stem and spread out into a fan shape. Place the strawberry fan in the center of the dessert. Chill at least 2 hours before serving.

FROZEN STRAWBERRY PIE

0 grams fat
without
crust

Serves 6

Prep   :20
Cook   :00
Stand   4:00
Total   4:20

1 (9-inch) crumb crust
1 (4-ounce) package fat-free cream cheese, at room temperature
1 (14-ounce) can fat-free sweetened condensed milk (*not* evaporated milk)
2½ cups fresh strawberries, rinsed, drained, and mashed to about 1½ cups prepared berries (reserve 3 or 4 whole berries for garnish)
3 tablespoons lemon juice
1 (12-ounce) package frozen fat-free whipped topping, thawed

Prepare the crumb crust recipe on page 212. Bake as directed and set aside.

Place the softened cream cheese in a mixing bowl. With a wire whisk, carefully start creaming the cheese; add the condensed milk and stir until well blended. Add the mashed strawberries and lemon juice.

Fold in the whipped topping until nicely mixed. Pour into the prepared crust. Place in the freezer for at least 4 hours or until firm.

Remove from the freezer about 5 to 10 minutes before serving. Garnish with a fresh strawberry half on top.

BLUEBERRY HILL DELIGHT

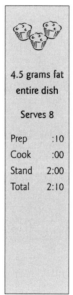

1 (20-ounce) can blueberry pie filling
1 (8-ounce) package fat-free cream cheese, at room temperature
1 (14-ounce) can fat-free sweetened condensed milk (*not* evaporated milk)
1 teaspoon vanilla extract
4 ounces fat-free frozen whipped topping, thawed
1 (9-inch) baked crumb crust

4.5 grams fat
entire dish

Serves 8

Prep	:10
Cook	:00
Stand	2:00
Total	2:10

Empty the pie filling into a strainer or sieve. Shake the strainer just a little and it will cause the thick filling to drain. Do not rinse. When about ¾ of the sauce over the blueberries is off, place in a mixing bowl and set aside.

Combine the cream cheese and sweetened condensed milk; stir with a whisk until blended. Add the vanilla; stir to mix. Fold in the blueberries, being careful not to crush the berries. Fold in the whipped topping. When blended, pour into the prepared crust. Smooth the surface.

Place in the freezer for about 2 hours, set out about 15 minutes before serving.

(recipe continues)

Variation:

> Use cherry pie filling instead of blueberry, but then you will have Cherry Hill Delight. It is a nice red-colored dessert for holidays.

SUMMER BREEZE

It's a breeze.

Very low fat, according to crust used.

Serves 8

Prep	:25
Cook	:00
Stand	4:00
Total:	4:25

1 graham cracker crust (page 213)
1 pint fat-free strawberry ice cream or frozen yogurt, softened
1 pint pineapple sherbet, softened
2 cups fat-free frozen whipped topping, thawed
1 cup cherry pie filling or pineapple pie filling

Prepare the crust according to the recipe.

Spread the ice cream evenly over the bottom of the crust.

Spread the sherbet evenly over the ice cream. Return to the freezer for at least 4 hours.

Spread the whipped topping evenly over the frozen sherbet. Return to the freezer.

About 35 to 45 minutes before time to serve, place the pie filling on top of the whipped topping, either in dollops or spread evenly, your choice; just make it attractively assembled. Place in the refrigerator until time to serve.

GRASSHOPPER PIE

4 cups fat-free vanilla ice cream or frozen yogurt, softened
⅔ cup thawed lemonade concentrate, undiluted
¼ cup tequila
2 tablespoons triple sec
2 or 3 drops green food coloring
1 (9-inch) graham cracker crust (page 213), or your favorite crust

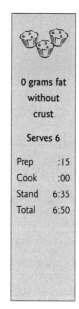

0 grams fat
without
crust

Serves 6

Prep	:15
Cook	:00
Stand	6:35
Total	6:50

Choose a metal or glass mixing bowl. Place in the freezer for a couple of hours before you are going to make your pie. Have your ingredients ready, so you can work fast. Alcohol seems to hasten the melting of ice cream.

Combine the ice cream, lemonade concentrate, tequila, and triple sec in the chilled mixing bowl. Stir to mix. When mixed, add 1 drop at a time of green food coloring, until the pie is the color of green you desire. Place the bowl, with your pie filling in it, back in the freezer for about 30 minutes. *Don't forget it!* Spoon the partially frozen mixture into the crust, smoothing to fill the crust evenly. Cover the pie with plastic wrap; return to the freezer for at least 6 hours. Let stand at room temperature for about 5 minutes before serving.

A pretty garnish for a frozen grasshopper pie is chocolate. You can buy fat-free chocolate toping at the supermarket and in Gore, America. Drizzle over the pie very lightly.

STRAWBERRY TRIFLE

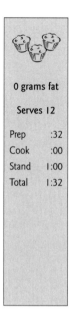

0 grams fat

Serves 12

Prep	:32
Cook	:00
Stand	1:00
Total	1:32

2 cups angel food cake torn into small pieces
2 (3-ounce) packages fat-free instant white chocolate
    pudding mix
3 cups fat-free milk
1 (14-ounce) can fat-free sweetened condensed milk (*not*
    evaporated milk)
1 quart fresh strawberries, rinsed, hulled, and sliced (reserve a large
    berry for garnish)
1¾ cups crumbled low-fat vanilla wafers
4 fresh kiwi, peeled and sliced
Fat-free frozen whipped topping, thawed

Layer half the angel food pieces in the bottom of a trifle bowl or a pretty, deep clear-glass serving bowl.

In a mixing bowl, combine the pudding mixes and fat-free milk. With a wire whisk, stir until the pudding starts to thicken. Add the condensed milk; continue to stir until well blended and thickened. Pour half the pudding mixture over the layer of cake.

Spread half the sliced strawberries over the layer of pudding. Sprinkle half the cookie crumbs over the strawberries.

Stand a circle of kiwi fruit slices up around the outside edge of the bowl and layer the remainder over the crumbs.

Pour the remaining pudding mixture over the kiwi. Top with the remaining strawberries. Sprinkle the remaining cookie crumbs over the strawberries.

Garnish with whipped topping dolloped around or spread evenly over. Place a whole strawberry in the center. Chill until time of serving.

LEMON LADY KILLER DESSERT

For this dessert I use a trifle bowl on a stand. It is a beautiful dish and so very good.

2 (4-ounce) packages instant lemon gelatin dessert
3½ cups fat-free milk
1½ cups berries or bite-size pieces of fruit
2 tablespoons sugar
½ cup lemon-flavored yogurt
1 (8-ounce) container fat-free frozen whipped topping, thawed
1 angel food cake
4 tablespoons coconut amaretto

0 grams fat

Serves 12

Prep	:43
Cook	:00
Stand	2:00
Total:	2:43

In a bowl, combine the dessert mix with the milk. Stir with a wire whisk until the pudding starts to thicken. Refrigerate for 1 hour.

Meanwhile, mix the berries and sugar; set aside. In a separate bowl, fold the yogurt into the whipped topping and set aside.

Cut the cake into ¼-inch cubes. Fold the cubes into half the chilled pudding. Reserve the remaining pudding.

To assemble the dessert:

Put half the cake-pudding mixture in the bottom of a trifle bowl or other deep clear-glass serving dish. Drizzle with half the amaretto and top with half the berry mixture. Repeat the layers and top with the whipped topping. Spoon on dollops of the reserved pudding and swirl them around for a decorative effect. Chill for 2 hours.

When serving, use 2 serving utensils. Dip them straight up and down to be sure each serving includes all the flavors.

PARFAITS

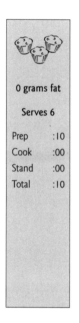

0 grams fat

Serves 6

Prep	:10
Cook	:00
Stand	:00
Total	:10

This is a quick and pretty dessert you can serve for everyday or for your fanciest dinner party.

If you are like me and do not have parfait glasses, you will probably want to do just like I do and use wine glasses — or any type of glass will do if you do not have wine glasses. Don't let the fact that you do not have one particular item stop you from entertaining or enjoying life. Dad used to tell me to "Make do," or "Use your head. If you don't, you might as well have two rear ends." Choose your weapon (glass) and let's get to it; it will only take a minute or two.

Fat-free ice cream topping
1 fat-free angel food cake
1 quart nonfat ice cream or yogurt
Fruit of your choice if desired

Have your glasses sparkling clean. This adds a lot of eye appeal—very important in food presentation.

Place about 1 tablespoon of the ice cream topping in the bottom of each of 6 glasses. Be careful not to smear it up the glass (remember: eye appeal).

Next: Crumble up or tear into very small pieces 1 chunk of cake for each serving. You be the judge of how large a piece—it depends on how large your glass. Place half the cake pieces over the sauce in each glass.

Next: Top with a scoop of ice cream or yogurt. Place about 1 tablespoon of sauce over the ice cream.

Repeat the cake layer and ice cream layer topped with sauce. You may want to add some cut-up fresh fruit. If so, put the fruit between the cake and sauce. Save one small piece of fruit to top the parfait with, or you may want to have some mint leaves to top your dessert with. Very pretty.

These can be made ahead and placed in the freezer. Set out about 10 minutes before serving, or transfer to the refrigerator about the time you start serving your dinner. If you do freeze ahead of time, omit the fruit and just add to the top at the time of serving.

LEMONY GRANOLA PARFAITS

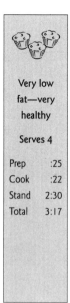

Very low
fat—very
healthy

Serves 4

Prep	:25
Cook	:22
Stand	2:30
Total	3:17

1 cup quick-cooking rolled oats
2 tablespoons honey
2 tablespoons sliced almonds
2 tablespoons toasted wheat germ
1 tablespoon flaked coconut
2 tablespoons raisins
1 (16-ounce) container lemon-flavored nonfat yogurt
½ cup fresh or frozen blueberries, thawed
2 kiwi fruits, pared and sliced
1 (16-ounce) container fat-free cottage cheese
4 whole strawberries (fresh or frozen), thawed and sliced

Preheat the oven to 300 degrees. In a small bowl combine the oats and honey. Sprinkle the mixture evenly over a 15½ x 10½-inch jelly roll pan. Toast the oat mixture in the oven for about 12 minutes, stirring frequently, until browned. Be careful to watch closely—don't let them scorch. Add the almonds to the pan and continue to toast for an additional 10 minutes, stirring frequently. (This part can be done ahead of time and stored in sealed container.)

Remove from the oven, pour into a small bowl, and stir in the wheat germ. For a dry chewy fruit, add the coconut and raisins while hot; for a softer fruit, add them after the granola is cool.

To assemble: In a medium bowl combine ¾ of the blueberries and sliced kiwi fruit with the yogurt. Spoon ½ cup of this mixture into 4 parfait glasses. Top with ½ cup of granola, then ½ cup of cottage cheese, dipped with a slotted spoon to let it drain just a little. Garnish with sliced strawberries and chill before serving.

STRAWBERRY FLUFF

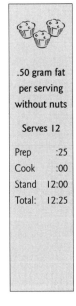

2 large egg whites, at room temperature
1 cup sugar
1 (10-ounce) package frozen strawberries, thawed
1 cup fat-free frozen whipped topping, thawed
¼ cup finely chopped nuts (optional)
4 full sheets low-fat graham crackers—not broken apart
3 cups graham cracker crumbs

.50 gram fat
per serving
without nuts

Serves 12

Prep	:25
Cook	:00
Stand	12:00
Total:	12:25

Put the egg whites, sugar, and strawberries in large mixing bowl. Beat on high speed with an electric mixer for 15 minutes. That seems like a long time, but don't underbeat. The bowl will be nearly full. Fold in the whipped topping and the nuts.

Place the 4 graham cracker sheets in the bottom of an 11 x 7-inch baking dish. Pour the strawberry mixture over the crackers; sprinkle cracker crumbs evenly over the strawberry mixture. Chill for at least 12 hours, or freeze.

You may want to garnish with a couple of fresh strawberries, whole or sliced.

STRAWBERRY FREEZE

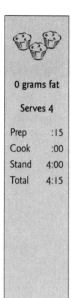

0 grams fat

Serves 4

Prep   :15
Cook   :00
Stand   4:00
Total   4:15

1 (10-ounce) package frozen sweetened strawberries
½ cup fat-free sour cream
½ cup sugar
1 teaspoon vanilla extract
Fat-free whipped topping for garnish

Process in a food processor or blender the strawberries, sour cream, sugar, and vanilla until smooth.

Spray the bottom only of a 9-inch square pan very lightly with vegetable oil cooking spray. Pour the strawberry mixture into the pan (if you set the pan in the freezer when you begin your preparation it will speed the freezing process). Cover with plastic wrap or foil. Place in the freezer until solid, about 4 hours.

To serve, garnish with dollops of fat-free whipped topping. You may also add a fresh strawberry or a mint leaf to make the dish even prettier.

PINK STUFF

This is a pretty make ahead for the ladies luncheon or church social.

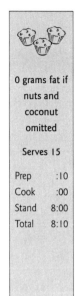

1 (21-ounce) can cherry pie filling
1 (15¼-ounce) can crushed pineapple, drained
1 (14-ounce) can fat-free sweetened condensed milk (*not* evaporated milk)
1 (12-ounce) tub frozen whipped topping, thawed.
1 cup miniature marshmallows
¼ cup chopped nuts (optional)
2 tablespoons shredded coconut (optional)

0 grams fat if
nuts and
coconut
omitted

Serves 15

Prep	:10
Cook	:00
Stand	8:00
Total	8:10

In a large mixing bowl combine the cherry pie filling, drained pineapple, sweetened condensed milk, and whipped topping. Stir until mixed.

When blended, fold in the marshmallows. If using nuts and coconut, fold in at this time also.

Pour into a 13 x 9 x 2-inch glass baking dish. Freeze at least 8 hours. Cut into squares and serve. You may wish to drizzle a topping sauce like chocolate or pineapple over, but it's not necessary.

INDEX

Metric Equivalencies

LIQUID AND DRY MEASURE EQUIVALENCIES

CUSTOMARY	METRIC
¼ teaspoon	1.25 milliliters
½ teaspoon	2.5 milliliters
1 teaspoon	5 milliliters
1 tablespoon	15 milliliters
1 fluid ounce	30 milliliters
¼ cup	60 milliliters
⅓ cup	80 milliliters
½ cup	120 milliliters
1 cup	240 milliliters
1 pint (2 cups)	480 milliliters
1 quart (4 cups)	960 milliliters (.96 liter)
1 gallon (4 quarts)	3.84 liters
1 ounce (by weight)	28 grams
¼ pound (4 ounces)	114 grams
1 pound (16 ounces)	454 grams
2.2 pounds	1 kilogram (1000 grams)

OVEN-TEMPERATURE EQUIVALENCIES

DESCRIPTION	°FAHRENHEIT	°CELSIUS
Cool	200	90
Very slow	250	120
Slow	300–325	150–160
Moderately slow	325–350	160–180
Moderate	350–375	180–190
Moderately hot	375–400	190–200
Hot	400–450	200–230
Very hot	450–500	230–260